CLOSE THE DOOR BEHIND YOU

CLOSE THE DOOR BEHIND YOU

On cyclical practising – a practice strategy
for musicians playing classical music

Morten Zeuthen

CONTENT

INTRODUCTION

This text is aimed at classical musicians, singers and teachers at academy level, as well as professional musicians.

The ideas on which the text is based have arisen from a large number of observations of both practical and theoretical character. My daily life, which involves teaching music students at the highest level, as well as my substantial personal experience of practicing, have given me the opportunity to test out this method, and I have been able to observe that in most cases the strategy works well. Moreover, I have for a number of years tested the ideas with my colleagues, who have contributed valuable theoretical and practical advice. I am especially grateful to Anne Gry Haugland, Associate Professor at the Royal Danish Academy of Music, for many good discussions about my project.

Like everyone else, we classical musicians must try to find new and better ways to perform our tasks, and we must improve and expand our ways of communicating knowledge. My hope with this text is to participate in this process, with a view to providing inspiration and contributing towards better practice.

But why is this necessary? If we look at the conventional practice techniques of musicians in general, we should really declare them to be a resounding success. The entire classical music tradition rests heavily and gratefully on the high standard of excellent musicians throughout the ages. These musicians have studied even the most complex works so well that, all through musical history, they have been able to enthuse a large audience, inspire ground-breaking composers and apply their own characteristic stamp on the compositions.

Every thriving artistic environment is of course in a process of constant change. However, classical music differs from other art forms in that the older music is at least as vital as the new. Classical musicians cannot therefore simply replace outdated skills with new ones; we must learn the newer music *at the same time as* having to live up to all the demands that previous eras and genres have placed upon us.

Moreover, over the last century, even stricter requirements have been imposed on the individual musician: one hundred years of recorded music means that every effort must now be made if the presentation of a demanding solistic work is to have any hope of being even slightly comparable to the recordings. As recorded versions of the works that we choose to play have become ever more accessible, our audiences have set their expectations higher, according to recordings of outstanding quality – recordings that moreover have been cut and edited to perfection.

These are some of the reasons why even more will be demanded of a musician in the future than is the case today.

Academies of Music around the world co-operate to identify what has been called "The Complete Musician". This is done in recognition of the fact that today, a professional musician, if he or she is to make an impact, must be able to do much more than previously was the case – and not just in technical terms, but also through other skills.

In previous generations, a serious musician was characterised by the firm belief that quality would always win out. As long as the purely musical work was sufficiently talented, serious and comprehensive, it would at some point be seen, heard and acknowledged. Today, however, it takes rather more than that. The huge media range of our times means that even the most brilliant musical expression may risk going unnoticed if it is not also communicated or marketed.

Now and in the future, musicians, in addition to a high standard of technical and artistic skill, must also possess competent personal entrepreneurship, great reliability, good physical and mental health, an attractive appearance, a broad horizon, personal charisma and effective marketing skills.

Consequently, we must find ways to learn our repertoire both better and faster – otherwise, we risk lacking the time and energy required to reach out to all the curious and open-minded music lovers that we know exist out there, but with whom we are unable to communicate to a sufficient extent.

It is unlikely that classical music will ever disappear entirely, but we musicians must choose wisely if we are to be able to convey classical music into the future as a popular and vibrant art form.

It has not been an easy task for me to decide on an appropriate form of presentation for this text. In the end, I have designed it primarily as an experience-based personal presentation, aimed at others in related professional areas.

Nonetheless, I hope that there will be sections along the way that will be of interest in other areas, and which will support purposes other than the declared one of becoming better at practising classical music. I myself have derived great inspiration from theoretical articles in related disciplines, and I have tried to incorporate these into the text where relevant.

Most of the work of a classical musician takes place in the practice room, and consequently, one of the central skills of the classical musician is the ability to practice in a fruitful way. A wealth of more or less well-tried methods and techniques are available to help us to master the art of "good practice". The method that I will present in the following, however, is not so much yet another technique, but rather an overall approach – *a strategy* – that organises practice (including its many different methods) into a clear progressive movement: a movement through three different 'rooms', each with its own focus, purpose and techniques.

I will describe the background and areas of application (parts 1 and 2), and then systematically review the three rooms. Along the way, I will also review a number of different practice techniques that relate to the stages of the process represented by the three rooms (parts 3, 4 and 5).

An important point in *Close the Door Behind You* is that the various practice techniques and learning processes each have their own place in the process of learning a piece, and that you need to work with a consciously progressive structure in order to get the most out of your practicing.

Close the Door Behind You is a cyclical practice strategy: I argue that we can regard the practice work as a series of circular movements with an upward motion. You could compare this movement to a spiral, or a helix: a circular motion in a particular direction, which includes the third dimension.

One characteristic of a helix is that when you have completed a turn, a new circular movement begins – but not from the same point. You have thereby attained a new level, just as when you ascend a spiral staircase. After each turn on the staircase the circular movement begins again, from a higher point. The method that I advocate here follows just such a spiral movement, and in the following I will elaborate on the arguments and on the application of the strategy in practice.

My background for writing *Close the Door Behind You* is first and foremost my long career as a performing musician, both as a soloist and chamber musician, and as a solo cellist in leading Danish symphony orchestras. For the past twenty years I have been a professor at the Royal Danish Academy of Music in Copenhagen, where I am head of the cello department. For more information, see: www.mortenzeuthen.com

For more than fifty years, my own practicing has been an integral part of my professional life, and as a teacher I have had ample opportunity to see which parts of the advice I have given to my many students have borne the best fruit.

In addition to my own artistic and educational practice, another experience helped to set in motion the work on Close the Door Behind You. A few years ago, I digitalised all my scores within the solo repertoire – more than 200 works. I did this in order to streamline my written communication with my students, and to ensure that I could easily bring my updated notes and experiences with me whenever I held a masterclass abroad. Each time a student that I do not know presents me with a piece that I may not have worked on myself for many years, I can thereby provide more qualified feedback on the basis of my own materials. In addition, the digitisation is my guarantee against getting into problems at my own concerts tours.

I put all the PDF files into a music program on my iPad, which, in addition to providing the best general overview of the works, also offers excellent editing facilities. Gone were the corrections, deletions and crossings-out of former days: it was now a simple matter to make sure that my scores contained easy-to-read and comprehensive notes, for example with regard to bowings and fingerings. In this way, the eye found just one solution for each passage.

When I played from such unambivalent material, I found that my playing was significantly more confident and convincing! This demonstrated to me how necessary it is to close the door behind you and completely stand by your own decisions. It would have been much more difficult if I had played from material that contained several alternative solutions.

I. INTRODUCTION AND OVERVIEW

CLOSE THE DOOR BEHIND YOU: THE THREE ROOMS, AND REFLECTION

You could regard the work of learning a piece of classical music as a task divided into three different phases, like a house with three en suite workrooms – rooms through which we all must pass in a given order before our work of practice can be deemed to be complete.

In brief, *Close the Door Behind You* is about how to pass through these rooms in the same direction, and close the door behind you each time. I call the three rooms:

1. The Laboratory, the investigative room
2. The Gym, the room for training
3. The Concert Hall, the performance room

In the following I will describe the method room by room, and along the way I will explain what you should do in each room in order to achieve your goal.

The work that you perform in each of these rooms is fundamentally different.

In the *Laboratory,* or the investigative room, you map out the nature of the task, its possibilities and challenges, and take all the necessary artistic and practical decisions.

In the Laboratory, all approaches to learning are freely mixed: logical and practical viewpoints are combined with artistic and personal choices. Reason and calculation are freely combined with emotion and associations. Stylistic insight is confronted with the musician's particular individuality, overall experience, and preferences.

Upon this composite and complex basis, the task in the Laboratory is to arrive at a comprehensive and detailed set of decisions that will solve both the artistic and the practical/technical issues.

After that, we musicians enter the next workroom and close the door firmly behind us.

In the *Gym*, we loyally practice in accordance with all the decisions we made in the Laboratory.

If the work in the Laboratory has not been done sufficiently thoroughly or carefully, it may seem tempting – or even necessary – to return to the Laboratory for a while. But with such coming and going back and forth between the Laboratory and the Gym, you can easily end up hampering and slowing down your practice process. Two or three alternative fingerings – or artistic choices for the same phrase – will become stored on an equal footing in your physical memory and artistic perception, and can end up cancelling each other out, or even opposing each other, when we perform the work for others.

In the *Concert Hall*
If, on the other hand, the decisions you made in the Laboratory are valid and have been practised as thoroughly as possible in the Gym, you may enter the *Concert Hall.* It is here that your practice must pass its test, and here completely different conditions apply, compared to the two previous rooms.

The Concert Hall allows you only one chance. It will weaken the musical statement in the Concert Hall if you do not feel convinced of the value of the work in the previous two rooms. In the Concert Hall, the ideal is for us to put all practice behind us and concentrate completely on sharing the composition with our audience.

That means that the doors to the Laboratory and the Gym must remain firmly closed.

In the Concert Hall, the extent to which the technical and artistic tasks of the practice process have been solved becomes clear. All the various elements of the work are brought together in the Concert Hall, and here we can find completely new inspiration and insight.

Once we have gained sufficient experience in both the virtual and the real concert hall, the movement through the three rooms is complete. (I will discuss later how we can create virtual concert halls.) Only then is it time for evaluation – for reflection. You must give yourself time to think through the 'concert'; to listen to the recording or watch the video. The things that succeeded in the Concert Hall must be recognised, preserved and enjoyed, and the less successful passages must be noted, analyzed and altered.

After that, a whole new cycle begins: You re-enter the Laboratory, but now you must examine other possible solutions to some of the Concert Hall's fewer convincing results and make new decisions.
Then a new session begins in the Gym, with practice/implementation, and finally a new series of performances in the real or virtual Concert Hall.
In other words, a new movement through the same three rooms, but now at a higher level and from a new starting-point.

Classical musicians return throughout their lives to the same works. The many principal works of classical music are characterised by the fact that they will always reveal new artistic possibilities when we re-engage with them. This is precisely why these particular works have been retained by the sieve of history as worthy of conservation.

We musicians will to some extent also be at a new place in our lives each time we tackle one of the masterpieces. For this reason, it therefore makes little sense to skip one or more of the three above-mentioned rooms when we return to a work to practice it again. The combination of our previous experience with the work and the personal development we have undergone in the meantime creates a new framework and provides some corresponding new possibilities. "You cannot step twice into the same river", as Heraclitus remarked.

When we divide our practice into the said three rooms, it is also possible to compare the extent of each of them. The three rooms in *Close the Door Behind You* usually represent three more or less equally demanding tasks, and we should organise our time and efforts accordingly.

THE STAMP OF THE CLASSICAL MUSICIAN

Our task as musicians is to vitalise and personalise the classical repertoire: to share our experience and knowledge of – and joy in – the compositions.

The fact that a classical musician rarely performs his or her own compositions does not make us mere conduits or copying machines. The greater the musical energy, artistic empathy and personal imagination with which we approach the work, the more strongly will the composer's idea be revealed.

Even if two classical musicians both strive to realise the same composition with the utmost loyalty to all of the composer's intentions, they will often arrive at two very different performances, because not even the most score-loyal musician can avoid some degree of individualisation in his or her interpretation.

This is partly due to the fact that classical music is created without electronics, exclusively via the medium of the musician's own hands, mouth or throat, with no electrical amplification or sound processing.

There are infinitely few classical musicians or concerts that can be regarded as perfect. Conversely, any product created on, for example, Apple's GarageBand platform is technically immaculate. This difference alone can give an indication of the degree of individualisation that the classical musician contributes at concerts. Such individualisation is an important part of the musician's learning of a work and is one of the reasons why the audience obtains a unique experience each time they go to a concert, even though they may have heard the work in question many times before.

ON MUSICAL NOTATION

The composer Richard Strauss felt he was able, using a well-complemented symphony orchestra, to recreate the sound that occurs when you pull the tablecloth from a fully laden coffee table.

A writer who describes the same unfortunate event can draw on far less ambiguous links between the written language and the surrounding world than is the case for the composer. The word 'coffee' may arouse very different associations depending on who reads it, but there is nonetheless an agreed core of concrete meaning in the word. This may be why the alphabet can make do with a considerably less detailed form of notation than a score in order to communicate with the same precision.

Accordingly, the musical score has evolved to become one of the world's most sophisticated written languages. In the same way that the letters in the alphabet refer to specific sounds, the purpose of musical scores is to describe a series of large and small acoustic phenomena. However, the score is also required to represent durations as brief as microseconds, as well as determining the exact details of pitch, volume, accents and legato/staccato ratios, tempo changes, and much more, to a degree that far exceeds the capabilities of the alphabet.

But although a score can be almost infinitely detailed, we musicians rarely find that we are bound hand and foot by it. The degree of attention at classical concerts is so intense that all of the choices that it is in the power of the individual musician to make can feel crucial. This applies both to the performing musician and to the audience. A small gathering of silently attentive people is quite enough to give us musicians the feeling that we are on finely-balanced scales, where we present our artistic choices with trembling hearts.

Much classical music has been performed a myriad of times before. So why, when the well-known classical works have been so thoroughly mapped out and digested, do they still form the backbone of a large, vibrant and contemporary concert life? The reason may well be the fortunate combination of the composers' detailed written language and the scope for individual interpretation by the musicians.

When we musicians try our hands at a work from the wide classical repertoire, we enter into a well-trodden performance tradition. But we must also decide for ourselves how that tradition should be used, and the extent to which we will allow ourselves to be inspired by it. Where will we follow tradition, and where will we deviate from it?

Perhaps the tenacity of the older classical works is precisely due to the fact that so many and so differently gifted musicians have, down through the ages, given each of them their often very different interpretations, even though the necessary starting-point – the score – is the same for everyone.

AREA OF APPLICATION: ON THE DIFFERENCE BETWEEN POPULAR AND CLASSICAL MUSIC

In order to see what kind of music *Close the Door Behind You* can best be applied to, it is necessary to explain a few of the many differences that exist between the genres.

One of the most important of these is the different roles that the musicians assume: Within popular music, it is the performing musician who is central to the work of art. A single personality can in practice present a meaningful concert alone.

The musician and the composer here are often the same person. Most prominent popular musicians create at least parts of their material themselves. Even when it comes to jazz standards, or interpretations of other people's songs, the artistic value of the concert is determined by the extent to which the musician or singer is able to give the music his or her own personal stamp. The value of a popular music concert thus lies largely in the originality and/or personality of the individual musician. The great strength of the genre is that it communicates directly from person to person, and that the music in one way or another reflects its time; in other words, new popular music is usually contemporary art.

In classical music, on the other hand, it is usually the composition that is the central work of art. Here, at least two individuals, namely a composer and a performing musician, are necessary to create a successful concert. A scored composition can in principle be a perfect and complete work of art, even before it has been played or sung. It is the score – the idea – that comprise the primary work of art, not the musician, as it is within popular music. An objective and completely loyal realisation of a written classical composition can in some cases prove to be almost completely flawless. The music must be realised in sound, and the classical concert scene is legitimised as a genre through the necessity of making the compositions acoustically available, irrespective of whether they are old or contemporary.

This division of labour between the composer and the musician is at least three centuries old. It was during the Baroque period that composers began writing works that really demanded professionals to realise them. For any musician, most of the central classical repertoire from around 1720 until the present day will include a number of passages – and often very many – that require a very specific type of practice that is so demanding that it must be deemed professionalised work. It is this work that is addressed by the philosophy of *Close the Door Behind You*.

The method is thus aimed at performers of *scored, demanding compositional music* – mainly instrumental, but possibly also to some extent vocal music.

In essence, the task must represent a challenge of a certain artistic and technical scope. Or in other words: If it is possible for you at the second or third attempt to produce a reasonably adequate version of a concert performance, you can safely ignore the strategy described here.

Scores written in the nineteenth century – the Classical/Romantic era – added several layers to the instrumental demands of the late Baroque, with requirements towards increased accuracy, virtuosity and timbre. In the twentieth century, a new layer of complexity was added in the form of new playing techniques and complicated co-ordination tasks between the musicians. Consequently, from the early Baroque to the present day, scores have become increasingly demanding to realise.

THE VARIOUS CLASSICAL GENRES
On solistic works, the domain of the major challenges
It is, of course, the solo repertoire that most exposes the individual musician. These works are moreover usually the most demanding in technical terms. The soloist bears the main responsibility for the

performance and therefore also has the greatest room for manoeuvre, and it is within this repertoire that you will derive most benefit from *Close the Door Behind You*. There will be plenty of work here in the Laboratory, the Gym and the Concert Hall.

Solistic works have often been composed especially for a particularly fine musician, or in direct collaboration with him or her. The solo compositions utilise the qualities that this particular musician possessed, and which might be out of reach for other, more average, musicians. In the history of music, the development of a particular instrumental genre is driven by the solistic works in the genre. Consequently, solistic works require a great deal of successful practice.

On chamber music: Make clear, joint decisions
The decisive artistic decisions required in chamber music must be taken jointly during the common rehearsal work. There is therefore a limit to the number of *artistic* solutions that the individual musician can maintain in his or her private process of practice, and individual practice must therefore leave most artistic decisions open, such as questions of tempi. One could say that the door between the Laboratory and the Gym can only be completely closed after joint laboratory work.

On the other hand, you should meet up at the first rehearsal with a personally worked-out voice, and with personal *ideas* about tempo, bowings and style. In the chamber music repertoire, technically demanding passages also frequently occur – the details of which must be brought under control. If these are not practised in advance and in solitude, the individual members of the ensemble will rarely have the possibility to listen to and understand their colleagues. Consequently, the technically demanding passages can advantageously be given individual study with the techniques contained in *Close the Door Behind You*.

The ensemble's joint rehearsals can also benefit from the cyclic practice model described. If an ensemble never reaches a firm *joint decision* on, for example, the tempo of the movement, the practice is doomed to failure, and rehearsal will be too much about the musicians' mutual disagreements, and only to a lesser extent about the music itself. An ensemble, just like a soloist, must be able to firmly close the door behind it as it moves between the three rooms of the practice process.

It is almost tragic when an ensemble, which has perhaps been engaged in building up a name, a repertoire and an artistic profile for many years, must be dissolved because the musicians have become tired of working together. When this happens, it is most often due to the working method being too disorganised.

A chamber music ensemble must be able to *jointly* do the following:
- In the Laboratory, find solutions to the artistic and interplay challenges
- In the Gym, implement and co-ordinate the decisions and achieve the necessary accuracy, overall grasp and homogeneity
- In the Concert Hall – whether virtual or real – unite all the details into a confident and inspired whole

After that, the musicians must evaluate the concert together, and then start again from the beginning – passing through the same cycle at a higher level.

On orchestral part playing, focusing on the details
In order to gain a permanent place in a professional orchestra, you must first pass an audition. This type of audition consists of at least two very different disciplines: one is a major solo task – a task that must be fully studied, as though it were to be played at an actual concert.

On top of this comes orchestral excerpts – a discipline that has become a permanent part of orchestral auditions over the past thirty to forty years. Prior to the auditions – usually a few weeks in advance – the orchestras send out a number of excerpts from the orchestral repertoire. Some excerpts are frequently used, while others are rarely played.

As with the solo repertoire, the orchestral excerpts that are sent to the audition candidates are often quite demanding. With orchestral excerpts, the goal is to illuminate the candidate's solutions to given specific technical and tonal challenges, and only to a lesser extent to focus on the candidate's own artistic decisions. That is the task of the conductor.

These very specific demands towards the standard of *craftsmanship* of the individual orchestra musician are so high today that at academies of music around the world, we are increasingly seeing the need to refine the craftsmanship relating to the playing of orchestral excerpts, in particular. This reveals the extent of the musician's ability, knowledge and will to realise a carefully defined task.

An orchestral excerpt for a string player might for example consist of six lines from the andante of Beethoven's Fifth Symphony, thirty seconds from Mozart's *The Marriage of Figaro*, or one minute from Mendelssohn's *A Midsummer Night's Dream*. Here, the requirements will be specified in advance down to the smallest detail, and they must be completely met.

These few seconds can be crucial to the professional future of a young musician. In this way, the orchestra's audition panel is given the opportunity to assess the different concrete skills of the candidates in a very short space of time. Such skills may include timbre, intonation, rhythm, stylistic insight and other technical specialties.

The orchestral excerpts may, however, also contain exposed *soli* for horns or solo string players, in which case the task is of a slightly different nature. Here, there is also the expectation of a more personal presentation – an individual commitment and colouring.

When you are practising orchestral excerpts, the amount of work required in the Laboratory is not particularly extensive. It is in the Gym that the battle must be fought, and because the musicians are, so to speak, playing away from their homebase, the task is determined by the challenger. At orchestral auditions there is moreover no opportunity to 'get up to speed'; the time available to the candidates to prove their worth as craftspeople and as artists is incredibly short, and the adjudicators have minimal tolerance of a mistake or a misunderstanding of the task.

So far, I have talked about the tasks to which the method described in *Close the Door Behind You* can suitably be applied. In Part 3 I will describe in more detail the three rooms of the practice process, but first of all I would like to describe some of the most important elements in the training of a classical musician.

WHEN WE PRACTICE

In order to understand what happens during practice, we must first of all try to separate the many parts of the process. This is no easy task, because practising classical music is a composite and complex task, and the many threads of forms of knowledge, methods and inspiration are often tangled together in an impenetrable whole.

Once again, one might justifiably ask: Why try, then? Gifted musicians have practised seriously for three hundred years, each in their own way, with fine results and without any recognised universal strategies or work methods. Moreover, all of these positive results have been achieved without the musicians concerned possessing significant information on how other musicians or previous generations have actually practised. Practice has been considered a deeply personal matter, carried out on very different instruments, by very different people and with very different music, and undertaken privately and in solitude. Accordingly, any instructions on how musicians should practise may seem pretentious and even superfluous.

But on the other hand, you do not have to walk many yards down the corridor of a music academy before you become aware of an urgent need: far too much practice is both unreflected and ineffective.

All musicians have experienced the difference between a good practice session and a bad one – some days can feel wasted, while on others we feel we have achieved a quantum leap, both artistically and technically. We should therefore try to understand why the difference can be so great in the benefit gained from two different practice days.

CONCRETE, WRITTEN, INSTRUMENT-SPECIFIC PRACTICE INSTRUCTIONS

Down through the ages, large quantities of practice materials have been produced, usually in the form of entirely instrument-specific books or collections of sheet music. "Tägliche Übungen" (Daily Exercises) is a genre in itself, which unfortunately in many cases calls for a degree of thoroughness that is completely unrealistic in relation to the time available to the student.

When a slightly desperate teacher writes exercises to correct all the things that his or her students have failed to master, the resulting book will often be much more comprehensive than the material that the teacher has built up in the course of his or her professional career. But in the rare instances when a prominent teacher has trimmed the material down to the required minimum, publications have emerged that have survived longer than the teacher's own generation.

The first important, instrument-specific books appeared during the Enlightenment in the 18th century, written for example by Giuseppe Tartini, Francesco Geminiani, Johann Mattheson and Joachim Quantz. Much of the redefinition that Baroque music has undergone in recent generations has occurred after the reading of such works. But the publications have not only been narrowly targeted at the individual instruments – they have also been strongly coloured by the author's personal preferences. At any rate, the works are mostly based on the author's own instrument handling, and they rarely give instructions on how students can get the most out of their own practice.

Musicians must find *their own* voice and strengthen *their own* technique. This raises a central question: How does a young musician cultivate a personal musicianship, and how can this occur while he or she is absorbing as much as possible of the teacher's expression, technique and knowledge?

If the art of practice is the key to good concerts and excellent musicianship, then it is surprising that this art has not previously been the subject of greater theoretical interest. For many generations, musicology has been at the highest level, both in terms of work analyses and in research into composers and their contemporaries. On the other hand, musicians have handled enormously demanding tasks – all the way down to our own generation – without the benefit of any scientific analysis, or even professional documentation. More than two-thirds of the literature that has been produced on the subject has been written after 1990.

One example is the work of Professor Harald Jørgensen of the Norwegian Academy of Music, who has quantitatively studied the practice of music students, and has amongst other things found significant links between instrument types and the amount of practice the musicians undertake. (See bibliography.)

THE INTERACTION BETWEEN TECHNIQUE AND ART

If we had had access to more insight into other people's experience in practising, we would be closer to being able to answer one of the big questions about the process: How do we ensure a good balance between the technical and artistic aspects?

A music academy teacher must be able to precisely balance artistic and practical guidance. For most teachers the artistic aspects will be the most interesting, since the teachers have put the practical and technical processes behind them. There may therefore be a tendency for the technical requirements for realising demanding classical works to slip into the background – not only for the teacher, but also for the students. Young musicians have after all chosen this life in order to play music, not to play scales and arpeggios.

But if, as a teacher, you wish to strengthen the students' ability to realise independent ideas, then in most cases plenty of time must also be allotted for scales, exercises and studies.

The technical issues are less artistic in nature. For teachers, the more technically oriented disciplines require you to work out a methodology, whereas the artistic side of the teaching rarely allows itself to be precisely formulated. The methodology of the technical tasks should include concrete instructions, not only on *what* to practice, but also on how to practice. We might create new teaching fora in which would involve several students at the same time and focus on the technical skills.

This does not apply to the artistic work. One-to-one 'apprenticeship', which is still the dominant form of teaching at the music academies, is a vital prerequisite for artistic dialogue, guidance and inspiration. This is because the artistic decisions required are of a much more plastic nature than the technical ones, as they involve to a greater degree various forms of interaction between teacher and student, similar to the interaction between musician and instrument, and of course because the different individualities of musicians comprise one of the most important factors in the appeal of classical music.

APPRENTICESHIP

Most of the instrumental and vocal teaching at the music academies takes the form of traditional one-to-one 'apprenticeship' – a form of teaching that has been successfully practised for at least 150 years. Part of this master-apprentice relationship consists of communicating so-called 'silent knowledge': One-to-one teaching transfers a wealth of information that is difficult or impossible to make explicit, let alone write down.

This sharing of silent knowledge is a highly complex process, because silent communication takes place via many different cognitive channels. Michael Polanyi, who was the first to describe such silent knowledge on a theoretical basis, wrote "we know more than we can explain". (1967: The Tacit Dimension)

But even if we cannot explain all our knowledge to others, it can still be passed on through apprenticeship.

In *The Tacit Dimension*, Michel Polanyi (2009, p. 4) wrote: "I shall reconsider human knowledge by starting from the fact that we can know more than we can tell."

The anchoring of apprenticeship in large amounts of silent knowledge is perhaps one of the reasons why knowledge sharing is not as widespread among academy teachers as one might wish. At the academies, teachers occupy collegial environments populated by their peers, yet it is rare on a professional basis for them to exchange more than commonplaces with each other, due to the lack of available presentation forms or platforms. In the past, the situation was even worse: the individual teacher's methods and insights were often treated like commercial secrets, because the academies, like the rest of the world of classical music, were – and are – highly competitive places.

The sharing of professional knowledge is a complicated affair, partly because the teaching of classical music is based on such a large amount of silent or non-explicit knowledge – and when it comes to explaining to the outside world what it all is about, then it really becomes difficult. But precisely because it is so difficult to give outsiders an understanding of the scope of the work that underlies a successful concert, it is also difficult to maintain the past respect for the highly refined professionalism of classical music. This fact poses a major problem for classical music and its future, since the genre is and always has been dependent on political and financial support. The processes that lie behind the creation of classical music must therefore be made visible, both to the general public and internally, within the professional environments.

Fortunately, recent years have seen the start of a very positive change: the collegiate communities have become more developed and documented, and this has created better opportunities to explain the processes to the outside world.

With the spread of the internet, there has also been a massive shift towards fruitful knowledge-sharing and new forms of collaboration between musicians – a development that has contributed greatly towards improving the educational programmes.

With YouTube in the forefront, the non-written dissemination of both simple and complex academic material has become much simpler.

On the other hand, the internet lacks quality control and experience-based recommendations regarding which videos or tutorials can best illuminate a given complicated scientific or artistic issue. It is a long way from the chaos of the internet to systematic and professionally valid knowledge-sharing. The new possibilities of the internet mean that the traditional concept of knowledge is simultaneously being attacked and strengthened; you can find anything online, but how do you know what to pay attention to?

Nevertheless, we can observe that the standard of classical musicians is higher today than ever before. For a modest fee and at short notice, you can engage musicians to give an excellent concert (even of very difficult works) almost anywhere in the world. The repertoire may not have become broader or more surprising, but the standard works are in general being performed to an ever higher standard.

Moreover, many new specialist ensembles have been formed within, for example, contemporary music and Baroque music. Today there are many excellent musicians with a specialised repertoire profile who are helping to raise the general standard.

The standard of the musicians has risen, but their career opportunities and fee levels have contracted. Today, as previously mentioned, a successful career requires much more than just playing well.

When my predecessor as professor of cello at the Royal Danish Academy of Music was asked whether a cello had sufficient sound to reach the rear rows in a large concert hall, he replied, "Quality always penetrates". This sterling but somewhat complacent attitude no longer applies. The enormous range of media available and the intense competition for the attention of the public means that for a young musician or chamber music ensemble, an excellent level of quality is no longer enough to establish yourself in the world.

We must therefore learn to acquire our repertoire faster, so that we have even better technical and artistic room to manoeuvre, and thereby also the time to devote some energy to drawing attention to ourselves.

We *must* become better at practising.

With *Close the Door Behind You*, I stand upon the shoulders of a long tradition of practice and learning in classical music. At the same time, I am attempting to meet the increasing demands for quality and efficiency by suggesting a structured and directed pathway through the highly complex process that is music practice. In the following three parts, I will review the three "rooms" and the movement through them. I will begin in the Laboratory (part 2), then move to the Gym (part 3), and finally the Concert Hall (part 4).

HOW DO YOU FORM A PICTURE OF YOUR PRACTICE GOAL?

It is implicit in the term 'classical music' that the music is rooted in an earlier era. The music has been played or sung by others before it has reached our time. Even much 'contemporary music' has in many cases been played at the highest level before we attempt it ourselves, and therefore – somewhat paradoxically – belongs to the classical genre. I will go into more detail about exceptions to this in the section on practising contemporary music.

There can hardly be any musicians who set themselves the goal of directly copying the interpretations that have preceded their own versions. However, the interpretations of other musicians and singers can inspire us and set standards. It is usually a prerequisite for successful practice that we have familiarised ourselves with the tradition of a work, both in terms of style and standard, and have thereby gained insight into the level of other musicians, for example regarding tempo, volume and perfection.

Perfection is the goal of every classical musician, but occasionally, the pursuit of musicians for perfection can cause concerts to become closed in on themselves. This trend has undoubtedly been magnified by the availability of gramophone recordings, radio broadcasts, CDs, videos and streaming services. Before the advent of the gramophone, opportunities to hear good performances of major works were restricted to concerts and were therefore rather limited. The great symphonic works, such as Beethoven's symphonies or Dvorak's Slavonic Dances, were, however, made available in transcriptions for four-handed piano, and both the scores and the pianos sold like hot cakes. The versions of the symphonies that resounded in the small homes were hardly perfect; these were in no sense definitive interpretations, but if at times the abilities of the musicians fell short, the imagination could at least be given free flight. The camaraderie around the twin piano stools was probably both humorous and inspired. This atmosphere of joint exploration of the wide world of music presupposed that the performers were relatively inexperienced and free to act when they set out to learn a new piece on piano, or as chamber music.

In addition, piano transcriptions were often the only way a large part of the music-loving population could become acquainted with great music. With the invention of the gramophone, however, it became possible to hear versions of the great works performed by the big names in music in your own home, and as often as you wished. In the beginning, however, only a few individual works were recorded. So, when Caruso sang, and when Casals, Furtwängler or Dino Lipatti played, a reference version was fixed for the first time in music history. In the shadow of these recordings, it demanded great courage – to the point of disrespect – for a musician to dare to attempt a completely different interpretation.

In reaction to this hindrance, young musicians were later often advised not to listen to recordings until they had formed their own interpretations, by reading scores and through their own practice. An authoritative recording could easily lock the free imagination and stand in the way of personal interpretation.

Many serious musicians still share that view – but perhaps time has bypassed this way of thinking. With the rapid development of technology, and above all the internet, it is now a simple matter to listen to dozens of contrasting recordings of a well-known composition. Many of these will seem equally convincing, although they may be very different.

Consequently, it may be that the time of the authoritative interpretation is past; it has been overthrown by the range of alternative interpretations, which – helped along by better technical possibilities for recordings and an infinity of editing options – are at least as flawless and mellifluous as those of the old masters.

From now on, individual musicians will be able to enhance their imaginations and insight by listening to many different interpretations prior to – or in parallel with – their own practising. In this way we can each, on a *both* free *and* informed basis, choose our own way of expressing ourselves. Classical music is like a language: you can only get better at expressing yourself by listening to and reading others who express themselves in a manner that is sharp, original, humorous or apt.

In the last generation, authoritarian musical gurus such as the conductor Sergiu Celibidache scornfully dismissed the musical tradition as merely an expression of spiritual laziness. These days, however, we can regard the tradition as being like a large, solid wall, against which you can safely play ball, because there is no risk of the wall toppling over. When the ball hits the wall, it bounces back at us challengingly; playing against the wall thereby trains both our musical abilities and our decision-making skills.

Concerts may be considered to be a commentary on the tradition. A precondition for becoming a classical musician is that you attend concerts and thereby familiarise yourself with the tradition. When you are in the same room as a good performing musician and other audience members, you will experience the music in a far more nuanced manner than if you merely listen to a recording or watch a video. The experience of what the composition has to offer its audience is more evident when you have the opportunity to sit and listen with others at a concert performance of music that you yourself are working with.

A concert is also created by the hall, the lighting and the sense of fellowship at the concert. To this must be added the musicians' demeanour and attitude, which can provide inspiration, and which can only be experienced live. A recording or video will moreover often be selected and/or edited, and this mediation also differentiates the experience decisively from a live concert performance.

There are also many of us who, with a certain amount of relief, have seen famous musicians survive mistakes both large and small and still communicate wonderful art.

THE MANY FORMS OF KNOWLEDGE IN THE LABORATORY

As mentioned in the introduction, the Laboratory is a very exciting and non-binding place to encounter a new work. But sometimes the necessary clarity and the required decisions just will not come, despite good work. In this situation it may be best to let the work lie until you have strengthened your general musicianship.

However, if the work ought to lie within your capacity, you can often benefit from trying out some new strategies. As mentioned, when you work with classical music, many very different forms of cognition are needed, which interplay with each other in an almost unpredictable way during the work.

As an illustration, allow me to describe a city: The piece of music that I wish to learn is like a city teeming with life and full of streets and alleyways, but surrounded by a town wall. I have tried entering the city, but the main gate is solid and locked, and has proved impossible to climb. So, I have to think about other ways in: perhaps the wall has a weak spot somewhere, or maybe I could try a ladder, a rope – even a balloon? At some point I find a way that works, and I can then enter the foreign city.

This is often how it feels when you learn a new, demanding work. *The many ways to occupy the city are represented by the many alternative forms of knowledge available during your work with a new piece of music.* If the most obvious method does not lead to the desired result, there is almost always another way to solve the task.

That is the reason why most musicians, if they otherwise have the time and opportunity, rarely experience problems with motivation to practice. If one strategy fails, then there are several other options that can be tried. And it is extremely satisfying when it succeeds!

Described like this, practising classical music could seem like a creative idyll. Nonetheless, musicians often find that concrete results are far too long in coming: Weeks or months can pass in intensive practice without you really becoming ready to perform the work. The technical problems may not have been solved, and the choice between the many possible interpretations may still be up in the air.

After a long practice session, it has often happened – both for me personally and for my students – that four interesting and committed hours may still not have produced any real progress. The problems are still the same, and there may still be too many errors, intonation problems, a lack of tempo control, incorrect nuances or stresses, and so on.

It is sad but necessary to note the lack of results. But we musicians often evaluate our work in another, somewhat peculiar way: we are satisfied with ourselves when we have merely been practising for many hours. But is the number of seriously completed hours of practice really the sole measure of progress we demand? It might appear so: We are often not even able to recall what we have practised after a few days have passed – we remember only that we practised diligently.

Could you imagine a surgeon, a painter or a plumber for whom the number of working hours would be the decisive measure of a successful working day?

This typical mistake is probably due to the fact that classical music to some degree eschews a tangible work structure, especially in the phase I am describing here, which I have called the Laboratory. Practice could not possibly, for example, be structured in the following way: Monday for fingering, Tuesday for bowings, Wednesday for dynamics, Thursday for phrasing and Friday for timbre production. It might look efficient and modern on paper, but for us it would be madness. The thousands of elements of music interact with each other, and you can rarely change one detail without it having consequences elsewhere in the music or the interpretation. We must therefore live with a certain amount of chaos and lack of structure during our work in the Laboratory.

So, what should we do? If we have problems controlling the wild hunt of the various sub-elements for each other, then perhaps we can try asking ourselves the right questions before we make a start in the upper left-hand corner of the score:

I have been given a task; on the music stand is a work that I have not played before. I have decided to learn it, and there may possibly be a date on which I will perform the work for the first time. Or perhaps a teacher is expecting to hear a good attempt at this work next week.

In the Laboratory, the questions we should then try to answer could include:

What is the style?
Which passages are hardest to play?
What is the form?
Which tempo should I choose?
Does it resemble any other music I know?
What is the musical texture, for example on a scale "from silk to concrete"?
What aspects of the work speak most strongly to me?
What is the most difficult part of the piece, and where should I start work?
What does the piece demand of my technique, timbre, stamina, attitude, overview, accuracy and memory?
If I do not fully possess the prerequisites needed to play the work well, how can I obtain these before I start work on it?

This list of questions may be either too short or too long, but we can save ourselves a lot of dead ends and interpretive mazes if we obtain the answers at least to some of them before we begin.

The order in which I have listed the questions above is random, because during the work in the Laboratory, as mentioned, I find that various large and small details interfere with each other, in an unpredictable dynamic process.

Unfortunately, it can happen that the practice process gets bogged down along the way. Although you continue to practice diligently, and even if your motivation is high, you may end up with the feeling of trying to build a tower from loose sand.

The sub-elements are interdependent, like bricks in a wall – we must learn to enhance our ability to place them securely, so that the wall can withstand pressure.

IMPULSES, INTUITION AND EMOTION

I have previously argued that classical music, although the musician has rarely composed the work himself or herself, is strongly influenced by individual interpretation. The fact that the performance always carries the personal stamp of the musician is, of course, one of the reasons for the survival of the genre.

To support this assumption, we can observe the strikingly limited spread of electronic music, with concerts performed with no musicians on stage. Purely electronic compositional music can hold arbitrarily many layers and may be infinitely nuanced, and therefore at least as interesting compositionally as music played by musicians. A piece of electronic music will also reflect the composer's intentions far more accurately than when a musician so to speak interposes himself or herself between the composer and the audience.

Nonetheless, the electronic music genre has had a very hard time establishing an independent concert platform and an audience. This is probably because electronic music completely lacks the individualisation that live musicians can bring to a composition.

What, then, characterises the musician's individualised contribution?

A good musician has an extensive toolbox of technical skills, experience, individuality and knowledge. Each musician chooses their own details.

For a string player, the details might relate to the choice of bowings and fingerings, bow distribution, vibrato, contact point, and so on. For a singer, the decisions may involve such factors as phrasing, breathing, registers, diaphragm and compression. For wind players, they may also involve questions of reeds and lips. For the pianists, it may be fingerings, attack types, weight distribution and so on. As mentioned, two different musicians will never produce exactly the same version of a work.

These specific choices that we musicians make are not in themselves decisive for the message of the music, but they become so when they are combined with the musician's emotional insight. Examples of emotional choices, based on feelings, might include:

When does our music call forth chills, or heroically rushing heartbeats, pressure on the tear ducts, mild smiles, surprise or anticipation?
What in the work appeals to my particular strong points – or perhaps a sense of tonal beauty, temperament, inner balance or drama?
When should the musician strive to surprise, and when, on the contrary, should we conclude? And when will we merely repeat?
When should the music dance, sing, rest or agitate, dream, insist, march or talk? Or cease?

We each choose our personal interpretations, because most of the significant compositions around which the classical scene is built contain a myriad of interpretative possibilities.

ON PRACTISING CONTEMPORARY MUSIC
The practice process in the Laboratory is, as mentioned, characterised by a high degree of freedom of method, and this applies particularly when we are practising contemporary music.

The term "classical music" includes, somewhat paradoxically, works written in our own time, and even premiere performances of new, contemporary works. This is because new compositional music is usually placed on programmes together with classical works, if we disregard actual festivals of contemporary music.

When you sit down to practise a piece of music that is not available as an audio file – perhaps for a premiere performance – then your approach and psychological environment are quite different to when you are working with your usual repertoire. If there is no previous tradition for performing the composition you naturally have an unfamiliar degree of freedom during practice, but you also have a longer path to acquiring an overall picture of the work, and to a good performance.

What is mainly expected from a newly written work is originality on the part of the composer. For this reason, contemporary music can often be difficult to access, both for the musician and for the audience. A large part of the original compositional means created during the twentieth century encompass new playing techniques and new forms of musical notation. Here, the ball is very much in the court of the performing musician, which often implies a great many working hours, since during personal practice the musician often has to master entirely new skills, such as complicated rhythmic notation forms, quarter-tone scales, or alternative instrument handling. Or maybe the instrumentalists are required to sing, or the singers to dance…

Much contemporary music also waives the idea of a fixed sense of beat for the listeners. In my experience, this is one of the greatest challenges in performing contemporary music. Accordingly, in order to accurately determine a musical sequence, the music must be noted down within an *imaginary* beat. The score is often characterised by a complicated rhythmic picture, characterised by polyrhythms and offbeats. Before you can embark on traditional practice work, the rhythm – or perhaps should one say the timing – must be decoded and 'internalised' in the composition.

In orchestral music, the rhythmic co-ordination is more accessible because the conductor indicates a silent (or imaginary) beat. This is a great help to the co-ordination between the musicians.

Within chamber music, creating perfect co-ordination – combined with an inaudible beat – is a far greater problem. Contemporary orchestral music and contemporary chamber music therefore presuppose two very different practice methods – a factor that far from all composers have recognised, and one which actually inhibits the spread of contemporary chamber music.

Classical music is 'handmade': the music is created with the aid of fingers, lips, reeds, voices and strings, and without electrical amplification or automation. This individualisation is an important part of classical music. The more famous a composition is, the more clearly the musician's individuality will shine through. When does our audience listen to us, and when do they listen to the composition?

When you play or sing contemporary music that does not have a performance history behind it, the audience naturally mainly listens to what is the novelty – to the composer. For the same reason, the musician becomes a more central person for the audience in the more familiar repertoire.

The fact that the musicians behind sophisticated and demanding premiere performances are very rarely perceived as being as important as the compositions may be one reason for the regrettable shrinking of repertoire we are witnessing at the present time.

Another reason, as mentioned earlier, is the increased focus on perfection. A premiere performance can never be as perfect as the performance of a familiar work that has been played many times before. If the classical music scene is to retain its vitality and attractiveness, it will require an expansion, not a reduction, in the repertoire of the concert halls, including with new and unknown pieces.

But this, once again, presupposes efficient processes of practice.

KNOWLEDGE SHARING BETWEEN THE LABORATORIES

While artists in other art forms can be autodidacts, it is striking that no really prominent classical musicians have learned their art alone! All of them have had teachers. An actor, a painter or a writer can create unique works of art without ever having received formal training, but no prominent classical musician has so far achieved success without first having undergone an apprenticeship on their instrument.

The part of the musical work that I have so far described relates to a strategy for practising. But since no one has learned to play really well on their own, it is also necessary to examine the conditions under which this knowledge sharing operates. A good teacher or colleague can of course make a decisive contribution to the value and sustainability of practice, but the form in which the teaching is passed on is crucial to the result.

However, books (like this one) with linguistic representations and instructions for the musician's work have never really caught on in music education. This might indicate that the cognitive apparatus of musicians is differently structured than it is for practitioners of other advanced professionalisms.

The classical musician of today must spend time gathering knowledge and insight, amongst other reasons because, as mentioned earlier, new skills and proactivity are required on the part of the musician in order to create a good professional life. We need to play better, but we also have less time at our disposal. We must therefore be aware of new learning platforms as they arise – especially in relation to the work in the Laboratory.

Digitalisation has created new possibilities for knowledge-sharing and new forms of communication that are much better suited than textbooks to work with classical music. Distance learning platforms and other closed internet forums can contribute to knowledge-sharing and inspiration to a degree that would have been almost impossible to imagine a few years ago.

But how can we integrate all of these teachers' instructions – and all of the YouTube videos – into our own, personalised version of the music? The more versions of a work we know, the more necessary it naturally becomes to choose or reject from among them. Only when all the important artistic and practical choices have been made in the Laboratory can the work of physically embedding the music begin. Or to put it another way: There comes a time when you can make no further progress by analysing, experimenting, reading, listening and watching; your choices must now be realised with your fingers, breath, voice and body. And this must happen well in advance of the concert.

Unlike technology, the human body has not changed in all the time that classical music has existed. What one might call the physical training of our musical decisions is therefore a type of process that it is difficult to modernise or speed up significantly, no matter what century we live in. This process takes time, and it takes place in the Gym.

III. THE GYM

WHAT CHARACTERISES TRAINING?

There is a difference between *practice* and *training*. All active engagement with instruments or the voice is practice, if we disregard actual concerts. Training, on the other hand, is only a subset of practice. The work in the Gym is that part of our work that requires the least amount of reflection and imagination. The decisions we took in the Laboratory must now be so to speak *massaged* into our bodies in the Gym. Body and instrument are brought together here in a fairly simple process borne by patience and willpower rather than by imagination, inspiration and freedom, which are the driving forces in the Laboratory. In the Gym, we attempt to unite body, instrument, task and mind into a single powerful unit, so that the music can convince its audience when the time comes.

My point is that any lack of confidence in the decisions that we took in the Laboratory will inevitably hamper the necessary work we must do in the Gym.

The working methods in the Gym and in the Laboratory are completely different: Irrespective of whether we are dealing with sport, physical training or music, the goal in the Gym has been determined long before we unpack our sports bag or instrument case; the target is now well-defined and can be measured, counted, viewed or weighed. This is in contrast to the Laboratory, where all paths and outcomes are open.

If a musician has taken well-founded decisions about the artistic content and the professional performance of a work in the Laboratory, then it is just a matter of getting started.

In the Gym, a musician, like an athlete, has no need of textbooks, the internet or teachers.

Think of the absence of human contact that we so often experience in the fitness centres: Scantily-dressed people gather together in a contactless community, pushing themselves to the limit – sweating, groaning and sighing. You could to some extent compare the work done here with that of a musician in the practice room: both in the musician's 'gym' and in the fitness centre, the ability to exclude too much evaluative thinking is often a prerequisite for achieving positive results. Evaluation of the work must be limited to improving your own measurable results. The music must be transferred from the brain to the body.

ON EMBODIMENT AND MUSIC

When non-musicians observe an excellent musician playing, their observations do not encompass any understanding of how the striking result is achieved. Some may think it looks unbelievably difficult, others that it looks like child's play.

Neither of these suppositions is correct. On the one hand, practising the piece has usually cost the musician a great deal of time and effort. But when you get to the concert, the whole thing can actually feel like child's play. This happens when, after successful practice, the body has so to speak built up its own memory of the piece. The patterns of movement have been so thoroughly incorporated that they can be activated with maximum confidence, even without the intervention of the brain or the will.

The body remembers.

If we are to attempt to understand how the body gradually absorbs the movements that the score, the brain, the will and the emotions set in motion in the Laboratory, then the concept of embodiment, and the theoretical framework that underpins it, is absolutely crucial.

How is it that we can carry out composite and complex processes, even though we are no longer consciously directing their execution? This is not a matter of a simple knee reflex or a sneeze, but rather a vast quantity of precisely timed movements, often carried out over extended sequences.
We ask ourselves: Is there a small, secret, reserve brain located somewhere in the body that can remember and take over when our consciousness is disconnected?

Embodiment theories have been developed over the past 20 years in a wide range of subjects and subject areas, and they have rejected the notion of the sovereign role of the brain in the learning processes. It turns out that the brain is not the only part of we that is able to control, recognise, experience and learn, as was thought in the past. Learning can also go in the other direction, when the body controls and teaches the brain. The brain, then, does not possess an unquestionable blueprint for our practice, but is influenced and taught by the body and the senses. René Descartes' idea that mental activity is independent of the body's movements has been refuted, or even reversed, through the idea of embodiment.

With the theory of embodiment, René Descartes' idea that mental activity is of a separate order from body movement is refuted and, in fact reversed.

In his article *The Tacit Dimension* (2009), Michael Polanyi emphasises that knowledge is initially created through bodily and sensory perception.
The Norwegian cellist Tanja Orning references Polanyi as follows: (Journal for Research in Arts and Sports Education, Nov. 2017)

This applies to both practice and performance, and he (Polanyi) focuses on the way theoretical and formal knowledge rest on the dimension of experience. He emphasizes that knowledge resides in the body and that the brain knows the world primarily through perception. After using equipment or tools to explore something for a while, we begin to feel not the tool but the thing through the tool. It becomes an extension of the hand; we begin to "inhabit" the tool, a similar experience to dwelling in one's body or clothes. When describing the structure of tacit knowing, Polanyi distinguishes between focal awareness and subsidiary awareness, which are mutually exclusive. "If a pianist shifts the attention from the piece he is playing to the observation of what he is doing with his fingers while playing it he gets confused and may have to stop" (Polanyi, 1998, p. 56).

Embodiment may be the key to understanding why practice makes a difference at all, whether the skill in question is piano playing, archery or cycling.

If we try to scientifically describe in words the movement and balance involved when we ride a bicycle, then our account of the complex interaction between the cyclist's physical centre of gravity, the rotation of the handlebars and the effect of the pedals, etc., will grow almost infinitely convoluted. In fact, the interaction is so complicated that it has taken years to create a computer program that can get a robot on a bicycle to cycle in a straight line without toppling over. The program is still not so sophisticated enough to allow the robot to turn the bicycle. Yet almost everyone has at some point learned to ride a bicycle, thanks to the body's unique ability to embed and combine even highly complex patterns of movement.

How does this learning find its way into our bodies? How is it being possible for the body remember, so that we can think of something else?

This is too large a subject to deal within this context, but at some point, the work in the Gym bears fruit. The key question then is: Why does a difficult task stop being problematic, confusing and exacting? How can it be that the passage at some point plays itself, without extra effort or deliberate focus on our part? You may have been practising a particular passage for 10 minutes, or perhaps for 100 days, but at some point, you have it. It is almost as though the passage has changed – it feels natural, it has been embedded in the body and has become part of your musicianship.

There are many different and interesting explanations of why practice is useful, but in this context, I will not describe the relevant learning theories, but merely give some practical examples of strategies which, in my experience, can create results in the Gym.

TASKS IN THE GYM

We can attempt to divide our professional focus in the Gym into three parts:

- The movements involved in the instrumental technique
  For the classical musician there are, as mentioned, many technical/

movement-based challenges. For an instrumentalist, a normal practice session in the Gym can therefore easily comprise 50-80% purely technical work. On top of this come the tonal and expressive parameters.

- The subjective expression
  In the Gym, we each choose our own balance between what one might call the "referential" and the "agitational" aspects of our interpretation, in the light of which we make our artistic and technical choices. What we strive for in the Gym is to obtain a convincing, well-worked-out, accurate and unforced version of the music – and of ourselves. This is where the composer and the musician become fused together into a single unit.

It is interesting to observe how this balance changes over time: Until some point in the 1960s, the subjective colouring of the music – the "agitational" aspect, the struggle, the dream, the commitment, the sweat – comprised one of the musician's strongest tools if the audience was to be swept away by a concert experience.

Subsequently, more and more emphasis has been placed on accuracy, flight, balance and respect for the composer's instructions, and a 'referential' element was more in demand in the interpretation.

Now, there are signs that the needle is swinging back again. Many young star soloists seem to be more liberated from the strictly score-faithful interpretation and emphasise a more subjective angle.

- The tonal
  In addition to the technical aspects and the aesthetic choices, we also work in the Gym with tonal colours and shades. Our sound is not only a phenomenon of expression, but also of technique and practice. It can take time in the Gym before the right sound is created. It is not only the technically difficult passages that must be embedded in the body – the sound and expression also require embedding.

In concrete terms, this may involve anything from bow pressure and speed to bow contact point, vibrato, air compression and diaphragm setting. The way in which we create the various tonal worlds is naturally very different from instrument to instrument, and so lies outside the scope of this text.

Practical practice strategies

While the work in the Gym is certainly a matter of automation and repetition, it should not lead to unconscious playing. This work also requires strategies, methods and finesse. The more consciously we implement our musical plans, the more we will get out of our work in the Gym.

In the following, for inspiration, I list some of the strategies and methods that I have found beneficial over the years.

Practising slowly

A famous German piano teacher is said to have instructed his pupils on the importance of starting any process of learning a piece by practising very slowly: *"Und wenn Sie dann in diesem Tempo das Material vollständich beherscht, dann müssen Sie es endlich noch langsamer spielen, bitte."* ("And when you have learned to play it at this slow tempo, play it even slower.")

Why did he say this? Of course, you always have to start out slowly if the score reading, the brain and the fingers are to be able to keep up when you are practising a new and demanding piece. But when you have learned to play a phrase slowly, why not gradually increase the tempo?

It was not the famous teacher's point that new challenges arise when you try to play an even slower version of the music, but rather simply to emphasise the great importance of practising slowly.

When you play slowly enough, you eliminate the confusion and stress that can otherwise arise when a wealth of unpredictable note relations written by the composer are compressed into a very brief space of time.

In the middle of such a passage, you can easily find yourself asking: "Help! Was it F sharp or F, was it the third or the fourth finger, was it an up or a down bow?"

If, on the other hand, you continue to play slowly enough, this harmful inner dialogue never begins, and you thereby avoid any disturbance. It is therefore wise to increase the pace of the music only very gradually to the right tempo. The mental derailments are avoided, and there will only be one version of the music left in your hands, heart and brain.

There are also many technical and physiological advantages in exhibiting patience by practising a passage slowly. When you practise slowly, you so to speak draw the source of inspiration out of the music. If you practise at the wrong pace, you are unlikely to obtain any new artistic or technical ideas. All of the details are fixed, the investigations are over and the door to the Laboratory is firmly closed. The benefits of practising slowly were among the things that inspired the ideas behind *Close the Door Behind You*. Practising slowly works!

But there is one thing to which we must pay close attention when we practise slowly: We must use exactly the same tension and patterns of movement as when the passage is to be played two or three times as fast.

If, for example, you practise a fast passage with great vibrato, that vibrato will make the passage impossible to play when it is to be played fast. The same applies to nuances: Instinctively, you play *forte* and in an accentuated manner when you are attempting to explore advanced sequences of notes in the Laboratory. By emphasising the music, you so to speak imprint it in yourself. But in the Gym you must leave behind the heavy playing style – even when we practise slowly – if it is not to hamper the final version.

THE NUMBER 16
A very large part of the work in the Gym consists of practising passages in which many notes must be played in a short space of time, such as fast sequences or large arpeggios.

When we watch a film, the eye is exposed to at least 16 frames per second, which causes us to perceive a movement as fluid. If there are fewer frames, we do not see an organic movement, but rather a series of rapidly changing single images. This limit of around 16 frames is the same for everyone but can alter with variations in brightness.

The number 16 is also relevant when we try to identify the boundary between perceiving separate sounds and hearing notes. Less than 16 identical sounds per second does not create a note, but above 16 we suddenly hear a coherent sound – a tone. Listen to the deepest note on a contrabassoon, and you can almost count the oscillations, at the boundary where the note dissolves into separate aural events.

Perhaps there is a similar, roughly universal, limit to how many notes per second our brains can follow? The ear can perceive faster note sequences, and the fingers can play them, but the brain is not that fast and cannot identify them all at the same speed as the fingers and ears. Instead of trying to follow all the notes in a lightning-fast passage, the brain must in this *case seek to identify patterns instead of notes*. This might be every fourth or every eighth note – you can leave the rest to the physical memory in the hand that plays them.

Briefly put, the goal of practice is thus *to swap the conscious control of the mind for the silent memory of the body*. The body does not suffer from doubts, but will act reflexively, if the desired reflex has been properly embedded.

When we have practised a difficult passage to the point where the body can take over, it is because, during our practice, the brain has gradually been removed from control. The door to the investigative room, the Laboratory, has been firmly closed.

Marvellous – but unfortunately the wrong versions of the passage that we have played along the way have been embedded just as efficiently as the correct version. Regrettably, the body remembers not only the successful but also the unsuccessful versions of the music.

A parody of practising classical music could be: A musician works with full concentration and conviction on a difficult phrase. This player then makes a serious error. Without further analysis, but with the energy of regret, he throws himself – perhaps at an even faster tempo – into the passage again and commits the same mistake. At the fourth or fifth attempt, he finally succeeds in playing the passage correctly. Yes!

Relieved and satisfied, he or she gets up and fetches a cup of coffee. This musician incorrectly believes that his dedication and diligence have borne fruit, and that he has now learned the passage, because he or she remembers only the last, successful version and has forgotten all the failures. But in reality he now has less chance of playing the passage correctly than before he began practising it. The many times that he or she has played it wrongly have unfortunately all become embedded in his body's memory – just as much as the only correct version.

As soon as you make a mistake for the first time you should stop and ask yourself: "Hmm .... Interesting.... What caused that mistake? What needs to be changed? In my next attempt, this mistake, at least, must be eliminated." The energy and enthusiasm we have at our disposal can thus be used in two very different ways. One is the "trial and error" method: Keep trying until you succeed. The other possibility is to engage our intellect immediately after the error has occurred, realise why it occurred, and understand how to avoid it in the future.

The first approach may seem energetic and committed, but it rarely works. If, on the other hand, we allow ourselves those few seconds to determine how the error can be avoided, then our practice session works.

As mentioned, the body remembers the unsuccessful versions of a passage as well as the successful ones. Not only do the undesired patterns of movement remain in the body's memory, but there are also often negative expectations towards this particular point in the music. When we are aware of the risk of failure, our focus becomes diffuse, and we moreover activate muscles that we ought to leave alone.

Allow me to attempt to paint a picture that illustrates how we can eliminate mistakes made in the Gym: If you write something incorrect with a pencil, you grab the eraser and remove the error. Then, with the back of your hand, you brush the paper five or six times to remove the remains of the pencil lead and the eraser fragments. The paper is now clean again, and you are ready to make new notations.

This is also how we should treat an error in our playing. Use the intellect (the eraser) to understand and remove the error. Then play this spot in the music correctly five or six times (like brushing the paper with the back of your hand). Only then will the error be removed from your body and your awareness, and you will be on your way to mastering the passage with no tension or apprehension.

However, it is important to emphasise that the method will differ, depending on which of the three rooms we find ourselves in. When we make an error while playing in the Laboratory, it is an interesting part of the necessary investigations that we make prior to our decisions. When we play incorrectly in the Gym, we commit – to put it a little harshly – a harmful blunder, and we need to play several correct versions before the unsuccessful version can be eliminated from the body's memory. If we make a mistake in the Concert Hall, then both the brain and the body will remember that we have "made a hash of things", and that will in itself entail tensions. So, stay in the Gym until you are quite sure.

How can we avoid tensions?
In order to be able to perform a technically demanding, high-speed passage with unfamiliar note combinations, we must make sure to involve only the relevant muscles. Tensions and blockages are like a spanner in the works – they destroy the flow and confidence of your performance.

To take an example: A pianist must, in a split second, be able to perform a four-octave jump – a jump of almost one metre – with 100% accuracy and without looking. The musician must in other words be able to rely 100% on the body's memory. This implies that the body's starting point must be the same each time the jump is performed. A slight, new tension somewhere – in the shoulder, the arm or the hand – can make the body unable to accurately gauge the distance, and the accuracy thereby disappears.

It is therefore essential to practise without tension in the body. The American jazz pianist Kenny Werner has made the fight against harmful tensions in the body the subject of a new approach to exercise. He calls his method "Effortless Mastery", and he has written a good book with the same name.

Kenny Werner begins the chapter entitled "Fear, The Mind and the Ego" like this: *"Some of us play as if there were a gun being held to our head, and there usually is – because we're holding it!"*

In one of his videos, he says:
"Now that you know that caring a lot leads to not playing well, you'll never care again – here people use to laugh. But no: Even if you know, from your own experience, that caring a lot leads to not playing well, the knowing that you are playing an important gig simply leads to sabotaging the gig, and you still won't be able to change it!"

For a jazz musician, performance pressure often leads to a lack of spontaneity and improvisational freedom. In this case, it is primarily *mental* tensions that hamper the musician. In the case of classical musicians, however – for whom the piece is already very well described and often technically demanding – we sometimes sabotage our playing with unintended *physical* tensions and blockages. The aforementioned pianist with the four-octave jump knows exactly what the goal is, where the particular note lies, and with which finger it should be hit. But if, for example, he or she tenses up in a new way in the shoulder, the jump will be inaccurate, and the error will be obvious to all. The mental tension leads to a physical tension, and thereby to a disappointing result.

When you practise slowly, you will probably not tense up. As the tempo is very gradually increased, you will find that the passage feels natural and familiar. The body can remember it on its own, and the brain can deal with other things, such as timbre or the interplay with the other musicians. Or the brain can simply be placed on standby for a while – being 110% concentrated all the way through a 90-minute concert is neither humanly possible nor artistically desirable. Just as the music needs be able to breathe, the musician also needs to be able to change mental gear if he or she is to avoid a complete meltdown before the work is finished, and if the music is to achieve the variety of expression that will make the concert interesting.

Those periods during which we can allow our body, our breathing and the composition to take over control are what Kenny Werner calls "the space beneath the conscious mind". But achieving this requires serious preparatory work and reliable experience. A precondition for being able to enter this mental state is a complete clarification of your own goals and means. We must feel confident in our technical and artistic choices. The door behind us into the Laboratory must not be constantly opening and closing with gusts of doubt but must stay closed.

Other practice strategies

• Practise in piano.

When you practise a passage in piano, at roughly the correct tempo, you will use fewer resources in your hands and arms, or your lips and voice, or your breathing. Not only do you relax the relevant muscles, but also the derived movements and reflexes, such as in the muscles of the face, shoulders and legs. When you master the passage at full tempo, you can gradually increase the volume to the level that you had originally intended for the passage, but now without adding new and inappropriate tensions. This approach is related to that of practising slowly.

• Divide up longer passages

If a particular, difficult passage is long, it takes effort just to acquire an overall impression of it structurally and conceptually. Such a passage should be divided up into clear parts, which should overlap. Once the individual parts have been practised, they can be recombined into a single whole. The body can remember each of them separately, which means that the only task that remains to the brain is to join them together, just as you would splice pieces of rope.

Hans Jørgen Jensen, the famous professor of cello at North-western University, Chicago, greatly prefers this method, rather than using a metronome to gradually increase the tempo of a slow version.

- Add a note

The "add a note" method is similar to the strategy above. It is not normally difficult to play the first two notes in a passage: you then include the third one in the flow. Once you can play these three notes together quickly, the fourth can be added without it costing great effort or extra tensions. In this way the sequence of the passage can gradually be extended, and often a passage practised in this way will feel completely natural and familiar. This is another way to create the mental clarity and physical relaxation that will enable you to avoid 'stumbling' over one or two notes in a passage.

This method, of course, trains the start of a fast passage rather more than its end, and one might therefore logically expect that the end will remain uncertain. But in fact, this is rarely the case. This proves the importance of maintaining our mental balance: If the start of the passage is flawless and relaxed, the chances are very good that the rest of the passage will also succeed – even if the end has not been practised as many times as the beginning.

- Use a metronome

Practising with a metronome is a simple and fruitful practice method that is not always accorded enough attention.

For what does a mechanically ticking metronome actually have to offer us? Any musician can easily maintain a steady beat without mechanical help. The metronome locks our rhythm and inhibits the organic and creative perception of the music. Nonetheless, we find that the metronome effectively strengthens the confidence of our playing.

I believe that the reason for the good reputation of the metronome is that it gives your practice a temporal certainty, an absolute *objectivity*. You can slowly and consistently increase the rate of the metronome to the desired tempo. Even when you can actually play the passage at the desired tempo, the metronome will enhance your security.

Rhythmically founded musicianship is also one of the best ways to gain authority in our musical communication.

• Transform the rhythm in as passage into something different

A smart way to learn how to play a fast passage is to pick out some notes that have to follow each other quickly, while there is more space between others. The rhythm of a series of quavers can for example be marked as a series of dotted eighths, followed by semi-quavers. Then you can turn it around, so that it becomes a series of semi-quavers plus dotted quavers. In this way you will play both mentally and in reality at a slower tempo, but your fingers – after passing through both versions – will have played all the note transitions in quick succession. This allows you to practice the passage both slowly and quickly within the same exercise, and you can thereby avoid tension when you subsequently play it at the desired tempo.

• Simplify

A rarely used method for achieving clarity and relaxation is to simplify a particular difficult passage. If at the beginning of a practice process you simplify a complicated rhythm or bowing, or omit some demanding dynamic instructions, you can later gradually begin to focus on more of the requirements that the passage actually contains.

We musicians usually build our practice processes up from scratch with all the details in place from the beginning, which means that it can feel like sloppiness or cheating to simplify the task. But the method actually works, and you can achieve good results by making life a little easier for yourself at the start. If, on the other hand, you try to get all the details correct from the beginning of a really complicated passage, then it may never really come together for you – neither conceptually nor physically.

The many sub-elements of the challenge do not necessarily have to be learned all at once. You can wait, for example, to practice a complicated bowing or detailed nuances until the bare bones – the notes – are in place. In this way, the body's memory, the musical understanding and the detailing are built up without any tensions or negative experiences being embedded in the body.

Children often practise this way and can achieve amazing results within a short space of time. Young children have neither the strategic overview of adults, nor their willpower; they just try something out to see if it works, and they don't get frustrated if it fails. If they are sufficiently talented, their music quickly becomes more accurate, possibly because they are too unselfconscious to add superfluous tension, but aware enough to know what it is all about. Young children do not evaluate their practice sessions in the same way as adults.

My point here is that "child prodigies" do not waste time questioning or reconsidering the goals they have in mind. They never go the wrong way through the doors between the Laboratory, the Gym and the Concert Hall.
Adults can thus benefit from being inspired by the practice strategy of children: "see if it works". I have found that there are actually passages in the cello literature which can only be studied in this way, and which cannot be built up in the traditional manner by starting slowly, using a metronome, etc. (This also raises an interesting question: Is there some kind of link between nonchalance and talent?)

ON CHILD PRODIGIES

You will not give good concerts unless you practise. But some musicians can manage with less practice than others – they seem to be able to take shortcuts. What do these shortcuts consist of? The central question is whether the shortcut is a question of strategy or talent. Perhaps the concept of 'talent' is partly a matter of being able to intuitively select the best strategy for practice?

A sober estimate is that it takes a really good violin talent ten to twenty thousand hours of practice – perhaps ten years of work – before he or she has acquired the necessary tools to be able to play a decent version of, for example, Brahms' violin concerto. But as mentioned, there are also extraordinarily gifted people who arrive at the goal much faster. These are usually children who are able to take amazing shortcuts, both in their learning and in their understanding.

Such talents are rare, and when they arise, they are unfortunately allowed to carry out their inexplicably lightning-fast practising technique with only their parents and teachers as witnesses. How interesting it would be if we could obtain better insight into what "a great talent" is composed of. What parts of the practising that other musicians must undertake are these great talents able to skip? Where do they start, and how do they safely overcome the obstacles that occupy so much time for the rest of us? What characterises the mindset of great talents, their physical ability, and their analytical approach? In short: What characterises the methods of the great talents?

My presumption is that, besides of course diligence, a very large part of such rapid, talent-driven progress depends on the ability to:

- Experience the music
- Structure it
- Think in new ways
- Carry out these processes almost simultaneously

An extraordinarily gifted child learns to play music in the same way that he or she learns to speak or sing. The child's approach to the task is rarely coloured by doubt. The musical and technical decisions are taken subconsciously, and at the same time that an understanding of the music arises.

Playing well is no less complicated a matter for child prodigies than for the rest of us, but the extraordinary talent is characterised by a child-like ability to have complete trust in your own decisions and those of others.

On a single occasion, I had the opportunity to listen to a highly gifted eight-year-old practising in the family's basement. Thinking that no-one was listening, he embarked on one of the most difficult works in the cello literature. He attempted – not without luck and with great daring – to realise his picture of the work even before a teacher had instructed him in it. It was amazing to hear how far he succeeded – probably because he did not doubt his picture of the music or wondered whether there were practical options for solving the problems other than those that immediately occurred to him.

Most adults are amazed by the speed at which many ordinary children acquire motor and cognitive skills. All children can quickly learn to speak their mother tongue, no matter how complex, and rapidly acquire the ability to ride a bicycle or write – processes that take most adult learners much longer, if we succeed at all.

Almost all really prominent musicians reached an advanced musical level very early on in life. The younger a person is, the steeper the musical learning curve.

In terms of motor skills, children, when they practise, do not build up tension in their bodies in the same way as adults, because their will and musical insight are only passed on to the muscles that are needed.

Picasso once said that he had spent his whole life learning to draw like a child.
The above-mentioned approach – in which we simplify a musical task and play around a little – can seem like that of a child. Perhaps it can also be applied at a more conscious level than that of children, so that we can learn from them.

THE ART OF TIMBRE AND PHRASING IN THE GYM

All of the practice methods mentioned so far have been directed at learning difficult passages and intervals. Nonetheless, in the Gym we must also practise the timbre and phrasing of the slow passages. However, unlike the fast passages, there are no specific practice strategies associated with this work, even though it is once again a matter of embedding the desired way of playing in the body. When we work on improving and varying our timbre and phrasing, we must build up at least as subtle a physical memory as when we practise the technically challenging parts.

Accordingly, questions of timbre and phrasing in our practice are not extensively dealt with in this presentation. But this does not mean that these aspects should not be worked on in the Gym, so don't skip the slow passages. It also creates some welcome variety in the work.

WHEN IT STILL DOESN'T WORK

Even when you follow all of these practice tips and more, things will not always work out as desired, and plans and efforts can sometimes give unsatisfactory results. We all know this disappointing experience: After having run through many successful repetitions of the same demanding passage, you leave the practice room with the happy expectation of being able, next day, to play the sequence in a triumphantly flawless manner. But it may happen that, next day, the passage *still* goes wrong. When this happens, there is a great temptation to go back through the door of the Laboratory. You would like to see if there isn't a better solution to the task, some solution that you've overlooked – perhaps a better fingering, or another point at which to breathe.

It may seem a little too easy for me to say now that this happens because we haven't done our work in the Laboratory well enough. But there is an exception to every rule, including our plan not to doubt our own decisions and our own practice before our journey through the three rooms is over. We may find in the Gym that there really is a decision that should clearly be changed or adjusted. In that case, we assess that there is no point in repeating a wrong decision again and again, with the risk of, on top of that, committing the error in the real or virtual concert hall that lies ahead.

But if we return to the Laboratory and change our decisions, we unfortunately also open up a small hole in our personal security. Every time we approach that passage, there will be at least two different versions embedded in the body, and the body will remember that we may have a weak spot right here. We may tense up inappropriately, or perhaps lose our rhythmic flow.

So therefore: *Wait a day or two before changing your decisions about a passage that will not come out right.* You may have lacked concentration, or you may have had a bad day. Or – most likely – you may not have devoted sufficient time and care to your practice of the passage.

But there is always the possibility to quite simply change your decision. As mentioned, there is an exception to every rule.

If a process of practice does not succeed, then, discouragingly enough, it is possible that the work is simply too difficult. Our current technical or cognitive standard may not yet be up to the task. It is a necessary talent to be able to set realistic goals, not least for young musicians. The extent of this talent is crucial to our musicianship, both in relation to practice and in relation to our concerts and career. We often wish to tackle the really difficult works before we possess the tools that these works require. Perhaps taking on the great musical tasks provides status in the eyes of our fellow students, or perhaps our longing for their musical values and technical challenges is so great that we begin the practice before we are ready.

One of the most difficult tasks of the teacher is to introduce the student to works that are within reach, but which at the same time represent challenges that students can learn from and which they have an opportunity to solve. If you throw yourself prematurely into a work that is too difficult, you will have difficulty later on in feeling that you have fully mastered it, even if you have actually learned it. The body remembers – somewhere – that the work was once too difficult for you.

KEEP THE BRAIN WORKING

The analogy between musical practice and a gym in a fitness centre has its limits. In order to derive full advantage from our practising, we must keep the brain working – which is not always the case if you are trying to develop larger muscles.

The methods described above all help to create a sense of security towards our concerts. Each of the methods has its own approach and its own logic.

Fortunately, there are many more methods than those described here, and most teachers and musicians will be able to contribute other, equally good ideas.

However, what all the strategies I have listed have in common is that they rise above purely mechanical exercise. The brain takes part in the process, and conscious awareness is brought into play. All of our practising in the Gym takes place in accordance with goals set in the Laboratory, and it is evaluated on an ongoing basis in relation to these. If, on the other hand, the practice in the Gym becomes too unconscious or mechanical, it will tend to tire us more than it benefits us.

If we possess the ability to learn the work, and if we have the necessary time in the Gym at our disposal, the question is how many repetitions we should aim for. Where lies the dividing-line between conscious and mechanical practice? In a real gym, the answer would be to aim for the maximum number of repetitions. But this does not apply to musical practice.

The famous violin teacher Ottokar Sevcik (1851-1934) recommended between six and twelve repetitions to his pupils when practising a demanding passage. Why this boundary? If six repetitions help, wouldn't 24 be four times as beneficial? However, experience shows that there is a limit to how many times it makes sense to repeat a difficult passage. Endless repetitions become too mechanical to embed the experience in the right way in the body. If you repeat the same passage an absurd number of times, you create a physical and conceptual reality that you will not be able to recreate when the work is to be played in context, and for others. This may be because music – when you play the advanced passage in a concert context – always to some extent involves our consciousness. This consciousness is usually combined with the body's memory, and if you have been practising mechanically, you may find it difficult to recognise your practice situation during the concert. In other words, an enormous number of repetitions of a passage may create a "bubble" – a physical and mental state that cannot be recreated at the concert.

Some teachers recommend a practice technique in which you mix the parts in a difficult passage, e.g. three repetitions of the first beat, four of the second and two of the third. You then take it from the start again with all three parts, in a new number of repetitions. There is not a great deal of logic in this method, but if it nonetheless works, it is solely because the brain is kept working and merely mechanical practice is thereby avoided.

In the Gym, we practise all the physical, technical and tonal details that we must master before we can present our music in public. But can we, while we practise, also anticipate some of the *mental* challenges of the concert situation?

There is a need for this when the red light goes on, or when the adjudicators take their seats, when the hall hums with anticipation, or when, as one of countless others, you are given three minutes to perform in an audition for a lifetime position in an orchestra. No musician can be completely unaffected by such situations, in which it may prove extremely difficult to recreate the physical and mental balance that we have worked on in the Laboratory and the Gym.

OVER-FOCUSING

In the Laboratory, we took the necessary time to clarify how we intended to solve the artistic and technical tasks in a particular piece of music. Here we worked with a *wide* focus area and enjoyed a great degree of personal freedom. There was plenty of time before the concert was to take place, or before others could reasonably have expectations towards us. The body was relaxed, the breathing effortless.

In the Gym we expect to see a gradually increasing level of accuracy, a faster tempo in the difficult passages and a more confident expression of nuance, phrasing and timbre. During this period, you gradually strengthen your focus on the upcoming concert.

At some point we have to decide that we now have confidence that our practice has borne fruit, and that we have come as far with the material as we can. But realistically, it may still fall some way short of a completely ideal version.

And this is where one of the most difficult moments of the process arises: we must learn to set *realistic goals*. If we fail to do so, and instead just increase our focus on the perfect recordings of our role models, then, quite inadvertently, we can actually harm our playing, in the way that Kenny Werner so aptly described.

A goal that is aligned with our personal potential and artistic horizon might be regarded as a sad artistic compromise. But such a goal can also be seen as the path by which classical music can return to the individualisation and authenticity that the venerable traditions may otherwise overshadow, because it brings us, as musicians, closer to ourselves. If we subject our music to too much pressure by comparing it to the performances of famous musicians and their interpretations, we can risk creating a harmful degree of over-focus. A colleague once expressed this in a slightly clumsy but accurate way: "Don't try to play better than you can."

When string players play with excessive focus it may for example mean that we play with too much pressure, especially in the left hand. A wind player or a singer may use too much air in a phrase, or not take enough time to breathe.

When we over-focus, we often try so hard to play well that we use up our last reserves of energy. Of course, we have to do our best, but we should remember that the best musicians always keep back a little bit of spare capacity, both in terms of sound and technique, and artistically. We never play our best concerts with our backs to the wall, or when we have no more left to give.

Another way to avoid over-focusing is to fasten your attention on something other than the most demanding aspects of the music. We could for example concentrate on the right hand when we have worked hard on a passage that is difficult for the left hand. In many instances, it all works better that way – because we place the task in a larger context.

To avoid harmful over-focusing, it is crucial that part of our attention is directed at what you might call *the big picture*. This picture has already been created in the Laboratory, and the clearer it is, the less likely we are to fall victim to tunnel vision and over-focusing.

Over-focusing can be a risk in any profession. Purely spiritual approaches are therefore also relevant, both in the world of sport and in music. For some time, Zen Buddhist archers have been a great source of inspiration in many diverse areas. After intense mental training, it is possible for these archers to let go of the self and focus entirely on the target. The aim is, by spiritual means, to approach the superior calmness and superhuman accuracy that these archers possess. They focus as much as possible on hitting the centre of the target, and as little as possible on their own person and success.

This approach to a demanding task can be a useful weapon for anyone, in order to help us to combat the kind of excessive focus on our own person that can paralyse our musicianship.

BREAKS AND MEMORY – ABOUT THE BOOK UNDER THE PILLOW

There is an old wives' tale that says that we will achieve better results at examinations if we sleep with the textbook under the pillow. It is probably nonsense, but the story has arisen because the subconscious mind is capable of working on a task more or less on its own.

At some point, every musician has been pleasantly surprised when he or she returns to a major task after having abandoned it for some time. While we may forget almost all the news we have read or heard in the past six months, the memory of the body is far more persistent. We frequently find that not only can we remember what we originally learned – we are often able to play a sequence better than when we left it several months ago.

What is the explanation for this pleasant phenomenon? And is there a way in which we can deliberately exploit the effect?

The fact that the subconscious can work on a piece of music on its own – when our musicianship develops without us consciously dealing with the issues –appears to indicate that we not only have a bodily memory located outside the brain, but that this extra memory is also capable of working independently.

In this case, the term "embodiment" acquires a further meaning. In fact, even if we barely give the music in question a thought, it nonetheless develops in our body and/or subconscious, quite without the application of our conscious will or personal evaluation.

Although we may have been dissatisfied with a passage or interpretation when we last played it, we have not consciously changed our strategy, fingering or interpretation in the meantime. And yet the music has gone on 'simmering' somewhere in our memory.

The learning that incontrovertibly takes place during a period in which we do not work on the task on the conscious level is characterised by acceptance – by the absence of doubt. It is therefore related to the mindset that we wish to encourage with the strategy in *Close the Door Behind You* – to eliminate our doubts and strengthen our acceptance of the music and ourselves while we are playing.

LEARNING TO PLAY OR SING WITHOUT A SCORE

A very special part of practice involves memorising the works. It can be something of a challenge to walk out onto a stage to play a major work without a score to support us. There are thousands of details that must be remembered and correctly delivered, within what is to put it mildly a tight schedule. And yet it is possible – thanks to the fact that we have at least four fundamentally different ways of supporting our musical recollection.

- Melodic memory

When we sing in the shower or hum a Christmas carol, it is the purely musical memory that is involved. We don't have to think about what note comes next – it just flows. This kind of memory springs from the archaic musical form, the origin of music itself. This phenomenon is the one that we must try not to interfere with, no matter when or how we work with our music. If we doubt our own abilities or the quality we have placed in our practice, we can easily block this particular part of our musical memory and inspiration. When we play or sing by heart, the melodic memory is usually the most important and dominant kind of memory.

- Physical memory

This is where we remember positions, strings, position changes, distances, intervals, fingering, places where wind players or singers breathe, and other details. When we play by heart, we must also remember several such details in addition to 'the melody'. It may seem like an additional burden, but in reality it is usually a support.

First of all, for a trained instrumentalist, grips and notes will often be so strongly intertwined that it does not "cost extra" to remember the grip when we remember the note.

Secondly, the memory of the grip can often directly help the melodic memory; if at some point you cannot consciously remember the next notes in the 'melody', you may well remember the grip.

When the music moves in small intervals, such as up or down a scale, the body can easily translate this small interval to a grip on an instrument. Problems of memory therefore more frequently arise in large intervals than in small ones.

When it comes to large intervals, the physical memory may be activated. The pianist must remember the distance and not just the melody, and the string player must be able to remember the new string, new finger or new position.
When we play without a score, therefore, much of the melodic

memory can be supported by the physical memory, and vice versa.

When we practice playing by heart in the Gym, it is advantageous to establish as many details as possible in the physical memory at an early stage, such as positions and distances. This once again presupposes that we have made our decisions, which is another good reason to demand confidence in the technical choices we made in the Laboratory. We must avoid having alternative solutions floating around like ghosts, because these also weaken our physical, bodily memory.

For singers, physical memory cannot be as concrete as it is for instrumentalists. However, some physical remembrance of the breathing, the adjustment of the vocal cords and the body will remain after practice. But singers do not have all the highly specific details of distances, fingers, valves, keys and strings. On the other hand, a singer has the lyrics. Lyrics are often as easy to remember as a melody, and therefore function as a good memory aid. Moreover, the lyrics are often in themselves a wonderful source of inspiration.

- Analytical memory

If a phrase is repeated as a sequence, for example four times, then the number four can be a simple aid to memory.

Another example: As soon as we have learned in which steps the basic notes of the subsidiary themes are located in the exposition and recapitulation parts of the sonata form, and in the major and minor movements, respectively, the movements become much easier to remember – because we have engaged our analytical memory skills.

- Photographic memory

Photographic memory is part of the spatial and visual intelligence or form of cognition. Some musicians can practically photograph a sheet of music in their memories, and simply read a musical sequence in their mind's eye while playing or singing by heart. This enviable talent that some musicians possess can be enhanced by training, while the photographic memory of other musicians is often so weak that we must disregard it.

We are now approaching the next stage of practice: The Concert Hall. But before that, I would like to mention an exercise that builds bridges between the Gym and the Concert Hall.

REPETITION UNDER PRESSURE

This type of training works well as a conclusion to our work in the Gym. Here, we combine repetition of particularly difficult passages with the pressure to which we will be subject when the concert has begun.

The exercise involves repeating a difficult passage a certain number of times – e.g. ten times – without making any kind of mistake. We place extra pressure on ourselves by deciding that we will start all over again if an attempt is not perfect, and that we will not be finished until we have played ten consecutive versions perfectly.

The first few play-throughs are like all the other work in the Gym. But the pressure rises as each attempt succeeds: At number eight and nine you so greatly wish the final attempts to succeed that the pressure is reminiscent of playing in a concert. As a result, you will often make a mistake in one of the final tries, and then you will have to start all over again. Bah! This creates an artificially 'risky' situation that will test your practice and provide good preparation for the concert, while at the same time training your technical and mental abilities.

PATIENCE

Patience is a prerequisite for finding the right solutions in the Laboratory. In the Gym, too, patience is a necessity to build up the confidence that we will need at the concert. Patience is in other words a prerequisite both to ensure you make the right choices and to create bodily and spiritual balance and confidence.

The only problem is that the music is not always patient. Music is expressed in terms of time, and milliseconds may determine whether the playing works and the phrasing is organic. When the day of the concert dawns, there is no longer any possibility of negotiation. The time, the programme, the tempo, the style – everything is fixed.

THE CONCERT HALL

We now step into the Concert Hall and close the door to the Gym behind us.

Many concerts feel liberating and inspiring. If we fully master the work, the Concert Hall can give us an experience of a whole new sense of freedom, in which the room and the audience provide us with new inspiration, insight and creativity. The Concert Hall is often where we discover new artistic possibilities.

In the Concert Hall, the ideal is therefore to let go of ourselves and focus on the part of the music that lies outside the self. Many people describe this mental state as "going with the flow". Here, we should as far as possible avoid judging our previous work while we play or sing. If in the Concert Hall we evaluate – or even doubt – our work in the Laboratory or in the Gym, it will inevitably weaken our concentration, confidence, authority and authenticity.

The truly successful concert is not primarily a matter of demonstrating our personal talent or successful preparation. If we have not closed the door to the Gym and the Laboratory – if, during the concert, we are still evaluating our interpretation or our technical work – then the concert can easily come to lack concentration, presence, authority and freedom. If, on the other hand, we completely cut our ties to the previous stages, then the fellowship of the concert will create an opportunity for us to see the composition in a new light.

But if in the Concert Hall we completely disregard all our decisions and all our laborious work in order to allow ourselves to be moved by new inspiration, have we not thereby negated the whole idea of *Close the Door Behind You*? Shouldn't we remain loyal to the decisions that we made in the Laboratory and incorporated in the Gym?

Yes, but the strategy is not an end in itself. If it has brought us so far that in the Concert Hall, we can seize new ideas in flight with confidence and conviction, then we have actually achieved the best we are capable of. The goal of the whole mindset is to *create the fundamental security that will enable us to express ourselves through music in the best possible way.*

Nonetheless, we must be cautious about altering technical solutions, in particular – such as the fingering in fast passages – during an inspired moment at the concert. This can cause us to lose our security and self-confidence and can lead to a great deal of preparation going to waste, as well as disturbing the audience's concentration on the music itself. If we play for high stakes and allow ourselves to be seized by hubris, we may risk turning our inspiration into indecisiveness. If, on the other hand, the balance between planning and inspiration is the right one, we will achieve the ultimate goal: an inspired and secure concert experience for both the musicians and the audience.

NERVOUSNESS AND STAGE FRIGHT WHEN THERE IS ONLY ONE CHANCE

Unfortunately, not all concerts are equally inspired and unproblematic, and all musicians know the tension and discomfort that can arise when the pressure is on, and when an audience invades our happy and private relationship with the music.

Today, young musicians have fewer opportunities to try out their skills in public. The concert scene has become 'professionalised', and there is a lack of the private or semi-private concerts of the past, where young musicians could test their work, nerves and talent in exchange for a good meal, a modest fee, and plenty of praise and encouragement.

Many people regard stage fright as an inevitable phenomenon – something we just have to learn to live with. If we play enough concerts, we will probably get used to it ... However, we do not need to blindly accept the harmful effect of stage fright. There is therefore good reason to try to identify the difference between the atmosphere of the Laboratory and the Gym on the one hand, and the reality of the Concert Hall on the other.

We might on the face of it assume that the tense atmosphere we experience in the Concert Hall is due to the strangers sitting and waiting to judge our musicianship. If this were really the case, then there would be good reason for the painful aspects of nervousness being one of the main topics of conversation when young musicians meet. However, in my opinion it is for completely different reasons that audience members put aside an evening or afternoon and buy a ticket in order to spend time with us musicians at one of the many large or small concert events.

The strangers, the audience, have come so that we can share the music with them. We share values – we are friends. *The phenomenon we call nerves or stage fright is rather due to the fact that in the Concert Hall, we suddenly only have one chance. In the Laboratory and the Gym we had an infinite number of opportunities to try again, but in the Concert Hall we only have the opportunity to make one attempt. This makes a huge difference! In the Concert Hall, our conditions and mindset are therefore completely different to the rest of our work with the music. And we rarely take this difference into account.*

Our best weapon against stage fright, besides of course thorough preparation, is our ability to create what I call *the virtual concert hall.* We must get accustomed to having only one chance per concert and must get used to performing.

There are many versions of the virtual concert hall. It is not a place or a particular form, but rather a mental attitude, a mindset. You can create a virtual concert hall when you play in front of a teacher, or when you make a sound or video recording. Even a mirror may be enough to evoke an impression of *it's now or never*, and to gain an idea of what impression the audience might get from your concert.

The goal is, in various ways, to test your previous work with the strongest possible visualisation of a real concert situation, even if you are not playing in front of a real audience.

If we play the same demanding programme in, for example, three normal concerts, we will almost always find that the final concert is more successful than the first. Only the most sought-after soloists play so many concerts that their music does not benefit by being played one more time in front of a live audience. But we can approach the level of experience of the famous musicians if we are good at creating an effective virtual concert hall around us.

If, for example, music academy students only have the opportunity to play in a concert or concert-like situation three times a year, then they will not in any way obtain sufficient insight into their previous work. They will not be able to appreciate the communicative power of the music but will remain vulnerable to nerves and other subjective obstacles and will therefore be unable to do their best.

PARALLELS WITH THE WORLD OF SPORT

Music academies around the world are experiencing an increasing need for research, therapy and courses that can alleviate the psychological challenges that affect more and more young musicians. For some students, the psychological challenges overshadow both their playing and their studies, for which reason there is a strong focus among students today on such things as psychotropic drugs, reflexology, hypnosis, acupuncture, conversation therapy and diet. While these may offer ways to alleviate psychological barriers, they do not in themselves promote art or technique.

Classical musicians, however, have many things in common with practitioners of elite sports, and the parallels with the psychological aspects of the world of sport have proved interesting for young musicians. There is much inspiration to be gained from the area of sports psychology that can help us to enter the Concert Hall with confidence.

However, there are also quite a number of contrasts in the demands that the areas of sport and art, respectively, make on their practitioners, and although there are certainly similarities, many differences remain.

In sports psychology, for example, athletes can derive benefit from 'positive visualisation' – a psychological activity in which you imagine experiencing a successful and trouble-free sports event. It might be a race in which you pass your competitors, or a high jump in which the body almost overcomes the power of gravity. This is often a good way to improve your performance and get rid of some of the tensions that can complicate your efforts.

But when a player on the national football team, after positive visualisation of his task, walks out onto the pitch to play an important match, his focus is not so much on the risk of making mistakes as on the chance of scoring, or of overcoming his opponents in some other way.

This positive expectation is not sufficient when a young classical musician walks onto the stage to play a demanding piece of music, even though there may be only 40-50 people in the audience. Studies show that the fear of making mistakes is significantly greater among young musicians than, for example, among elite football players, which might on the face of it appear absurd: If a young pianist makes a huge mistake in a Beethoven sonata in front of an audience of 50 people, the damage is negligible, and there will be an opportunity in the next second to delight in the beauty of the sound or the player's musical originality. Beethoven's reputation will not have suffered any harm, and the audience can still easily obtain a good experience from the concert.

On the other hand, it can often have serious consequences if a national team player makes an ill-judged pass and thereby creates a goal opportunity for the opposing team that decides the match. Half the country will be angry about the error – which hardly applies to a mistake in a Beethoven sonata.

Visualisation of flawless efforts in the manner of sports psychology can even, in my opinion, risk harming a young musician's performance. When we perform classical music, the sequence of events is pre-determined to a much greater degree than it is at a football match. For this reason, it is perhaps crucial that we are familiar with the many forms of nervousness in advance. Nervousness is at its worst when we are insufficiently prepared. It is the sense of *surprise*, not the concert itself, that is dangerous. Many good musicians have found themselves on the defensive even at informal concerts with a familiar repertoire, precisely because the concert's non-committal character has caused them to ignore the risks that are inherent in any concert – including the informal ones.

But perhaps the world of sport can help us to minimise some of the culture of fear that can hamper the classical music milieu. Like athletes, we must make use of positive expectations towards ourselves and our fellowship with our audience, and thereby relativize the fear of the less than perfect – an anxiety that should not be allowed to overshadow our positive overall perception of the task and the music.

THE HARMFUL INTERNAL DIALOGUE

During a concert, our brains always work faster than usual because we are extra mobilised. We should not categorise this reaction among the multitude of phenomena that we call nervousness. The extra mobilisation is predominantly a positive phenomenon, even if it feels alien.

When, in connection with a concert, we mobilise everything we have, we are able to perceive, react and think considerably faster and more intensely than we did in the Laboratory or the Gym. Usually, this will strengthen the intensity and confidence of a concert. We can for example respond more quickly to unexpected events with the musicians with whom we are playing or create a fingering on the spot if need be. We can perceive that someone in the audience has dropped his keys on the floor, and yet still retain ample concentration on our playing, because we are so completely mentally alert. This mobilisation can even create new inspiration, as described at the beginning of the chapter on the Concert Hall. In short, we are on our toes.

Unfortunately, this very mobilisation can also *harm* our playing. All of our good intentions can give rise to an unnecessary internal dialogue, such as: "Is it G or G sharp in the next beat? Was I in time with the pianist just now? Have I practised the difficult passage in the coda enough? Are people bored? Should I have chosen the other fingering?"

When questions like these arise, they can harm your concentration and your playing. The brain has become so fast in operation that it can run away from the timing to which the music is subject. As a result, you will not always be able to restore the standard that has been so carefully built up in the Laboratory and the Gym, precisely because the situation may feel foreign. Our heightened mental ability can then actually impair our co-ordination and our balance.

By getting used to the fact that in the Concert Hall we work in a new state of mental mobilisation, we can exploit this fact without being alienated by it.

ABOUT CO-ORDINATION

When we play well, several independent processes operate in a simultaneous and co-ordinated manner. These may be rhythmic, technical or psychological.

Allow me to paint a picture of this co-ordination. You could compare the successful performance of a piece of music to a team of circus horses running around a circus ring. The beauty of this familiar circus act arises from the fact that the horses run in co-ordination, side by side, as they circle the ring again and again.

Similarly, when we play, our task is to co-ordinate at least three 'horses':

The *first horse* is the objective tempo of the music. In classical music this tempo is rarely a purely metronomic unit but is the sequence of time in which the music works best, and the pace that underlies the co-ordination with the other musicians. In a hectic concert situation, it is not uncommon for the musical pulse to rise, along with our increased heart rate. The tempo horse runs ahead, and the performance will suffer severely.

The *second horse* is what we might call the subjective tempo: the pace that determines what we physically do. This is the timing created by our hands, thoughts and breathing. We must ensure that our technique corresponds precisely to the objective tempo, or else an synchronicity will arise, for example between your right and left hand, or between the various musicians on the stage.

The *third horse* is the musical focus, or the memory. This is naturally in operation when we play the music by heart, but it also co-ordinates when and what we wish to express musically. If the memory (or the artistic presence) does not follow along with the other two horses then things start to go wrong – most obviously of course if you actually get stuck. We rarely forget what we have been practising for a long time, but we may lose our concentration – the horse that carries the memory falls behind.

But the memory can also get too far ahead. We cannot, for example, both think about the music we are playing right now and the music that we will have to play in ten seconds' time. We often make that mistake because we want to feel extra secure, but actual errors can arise when the horse that carries the memory loses its place in the team.

When an important concert brings about mental hyperactivity, it often affects the delicate synchronisation of the musical elements – the parallel movements of the horses.

That is the reason why a metronome – despite its unartistic rigidity – is a good aid even when you are well advanced in your practice process, as I mentioned in the section about the Gym. A metronome strengthens the co-ordination of the three different mental processes, or 'horses', with strict discipline. But the metronome needs to be internalised – it doesn't look good on a stage, and the music also requires flexibility. Classical music may be rhythmic, but it is not rigid.

ON OTHER DANGEROUS ANIMALS

I have now mentioned a few concrete but very different reasons why we may play worse than we deserve in stressful situations. If we merely consider all of the problems under a single heading as 'nerves', we will be ill-equipped to combat them. They must be confronted individually, because they are very different animals – in fact there is a whole zoo of them.

Musicians who play wind instruments, for example, may feel dry in the mouth or short of breath. They naturally experience this as a problem, which may in turn intensify the feeling of nervousness. It may well be that string players also get dry mouths, but because this is not a problem for them they do not notice it, and so the problem does not become self-reinforcing.

Pianists and string players, on the other hand, may experience trembling or sweaty fingers, or tense up so much that they forget the distances on the fingerboard or keyboard. Singers may experience coatings on the vocal cords or lose their sense of contact with the diaphragm.

If we expand our familiarity with the many forms of nervousness, we can learn how to tackle them and make them less of a problem. If, on the other hand, we fail to confront the reactions that peak stress can cause us, then they can take us by surprise, and that is when we can really become vulnerable. It is when we can no longer recognise ourselves that things go wrong.

It is important to keep in mind that the reactions that we call nervousness are not personal, but universal. Here I would like to mention two different theories that help to explain why we often play below our real standard in the Concert Hall.

Noa Kageyama, in his blog "The Bulletproof Musician", which I can recommend strongly, describes two competing theories on why our focus may slip during a concert.

The first is the *distraction theory*, which is associated with the aforementioned harmful internal dialogue. The inner dialogue here may be about thoughts and energies that have nothing to do with our concert. You may be wondering what the audience thinks of you, whether your clothing is suitable for the event, or whether you have practised enough. In this way we start up an irrelevant internal dialogue that can obscure the focus points we established during our practice.

However, if we happen to think about our laces in the middle of a technically or musically crucial passage, this does not in itself necessarily have to harm our playing – remember that in the concert, we have mobilised extra mental capacity.

The second theory is the *detail theory*. Here, the negative internal monologue also plays a role, but it differs from the distraction theory in that, because of our burning desire to achieve perfection in the concert situation, we simply monitor our music too much. The physical memory and autonomy that we incorporated in the Gym can thereby be lost; in this situation we do not trust enough in the body's memory. If we suddenly make an extra effort with a change of position – a change that we have long relied on the body to manage on its own – then we may come out of our learned automation, and our practice may be disabled.

This error may occur because we do not dare to let go of the efforts to improve that we made in the Gym – we are still practising when we play the concert, and the door to the Gym has not been firmly closed behind us.

It really pays to try to distinguish between these two crucially different possibilities for distraction, which will place you in a better position if you briefly lose focus in the Concert Hall.

SET REALISTIC GOALS

When the concert is over, we usually pack away our previous problems with performance anxiety into a large black plastic refuse sack, like unsorted, unpleasant and incomprehensible events.

We may feel a little ashamed, either because we consider nervousness to be a sign of lack of talent or of weakness of character – or both. When we find that our concerts are adversely affected by nervousness, the reaction from other musicians is usually: "We've all been there", "It's part of the game", "It passes with experience", etc. We encounter great collegial understanding after nervous concerts, and after a beer the unpleasant memory is repressed, and we just hope for better luck next time.

When the subject comes up between teachers and students, the teacher often merely replies that he or she "can well remember how terribly nervous I was in my young days. Oh yes! Ha ha!"

But when we fall victim to nervousness, disappointment or tensions, it is often because we have set our ambitions and our goals too high.

We are probably more likely to commit this error than athletes, because music is subject to more complex and subjective assessment criteria than sport. This may be the reason why fear plays a greater role for young musicians than for athletes, as I mentioned earlier.

These assessment criteria are rather intangible and may include a wonderful sound, a strong personal fingerprint, a particularly attentive temperament, subtle communication skills, a unique personal charisma or charm, and so on... The demands can feel overwhelming, and there will always be things that could be done better.

But, conversely, we can also perceive this enormous range of possibilities as liberating. Since there is no list of right ways for our interpretations – we can prioritise the possibilities in the interpretations that best match the type of talent we possess.

If music were like sport, the evaluation of our concerts would merely be a question of measuring who played fastest or most powerfully, or most flawlessly. But music is not sport; there is an infinity of possibilities in our personal interpretations to create beauty, meaning and surprises.

We do not need to account for all of the artistic possibilities in the works we play. We should choose our own version, including the more 'sports-like' parameters such as tempo and volume. There is great freedom inherent in this, and this is a freedom on which we can advantageously focus.

Many young musicians fervently wish to achieve too many things at once. They consider it an expression of seriousness and knowledge if their burning musical commitment lights small bonfires of rage – including when they make small or large mistakes while practising. But this rarely leads to a good result – the small bonfires can often burn out of control when it is no longer a question of practice, but a concert.

Unfortunately, this risk can also be amplified by teachers. When the music professors of former times worked themselves up into a fit of rage over some minor blunder, it could look like burning dedication and seriousness. But the outburst could harm the pupils far more than it benefited them – it distorted the proportions of the concert and destroyed the necessary balance.

"DON'T PERFORM WHEN YOU PRACTISE, AND DON'T PRACTISE WHEN YOU PERFORM" (KENNY WERNER)

In the section on the Gym, I warned about the inappropriateness of attempting a concert version long before the preconditions are present for a successful result. The unsuccessful attempts embed themselves negatively in both the body's memory, the image of the composition, and the musician's self-confidence.

But it is even more problematic if we practise in front of our audience. In the Concert Hall, the ideal is to forget about the technical challenges of the work, and to base the performance on clear answers to the musical and technical questions that the work poses, and on the rock-solid implementation of these.

If we are to have any hope of bringing our audience along with us, it is not enough merely to realise the composer's instructions correctly and at the right tempo. In the Concert Hall, it is all about throwing away all the intermediate calculations and letting the music flow freely, as though it were the simplest thing in the world.

If, on the other hand, the audience gains the impression that we musicians are viewing the concert as a personal test, or as an extension of the work method in the Laboratory or the Gym, then neither the musician nor the audience will be given the experience that we seek to convey.

The Concert Hall is a unique learning space, but it is not a practice room. John Cage expressed the same idea in a slightly different way in a list he wrote on how best to teach composition: "Don't try to create and analyse at the same time. They're different processes."

HOW DO WE BUILD A VIRTUAL CONCERT HALL?

All classical musicians can agree that concert experience is an indispensable prerequisite for great musicianship. I have several times in this little book described the need to establish virtual concert halls as a supplement to our real concerts. In the following I will therefore present some more detailed ideas for ways to create virtual concert environments.

In the previous section, I described the role of nervousness, particularly for young musicians, and I addressed ways to eliminate many of the causes of nerves and tensions with ideas for better practice.

How many opportunities does a young musician usually have in a year to perform as a soloist in front of a real audience? The answer is of course: not enough.

As described in the introduction to the chapter, the concert opportunities for young musicians have been reduced, while the demands on them have risen. But we can do something about that.

One of the older piano teachers at the Royal Danish Academy of Music practised her own version of a virtual concert hall. In her teaching room, among musical scores and busts of dead composers, there was a blue coffee pot. When she had completed a process of practice with one of her students, she said, "So, now you play for the Coffee Pot", after which the student bowed and played the work for the coffee pot and the teacher, just as though they constituted a whole audience in a grandiose concert hall.

It turned out that it is actually quite easy to establish a brand-new mindset, just by focusing the attention on a blue coffee pot. Faced with the coffee pot, we still have only one chance. Our evaluations, excuses, minor corrections and new plans must give way to the decisive factor: the concert, or in this case, the coffee pot.

The famous teachers at the major academies have classes that contain a great many impressive talents, and it is these young people who often win international competitions. As a result, the teacher is highly sought after, and the competition to get into the class is correspondingly fierce; a self-reinforcing process. When the privileged students receive tuition, there is therefore something genuinely at stake, and the first note played after the instrument is unpacked already has the character of a concert performance. There are often other students sitting and listening, and any tendency to practise, make excuses or chat in the lessons is eliminated.

When you receive tuition from a highly respected teacher, this can in itself feel like a kind of concert situation: You do not practise in the teacher's presence – you are keen to show how far you have come. You play a concert.

Of course, these professors also run their classes excellently, and often hit exactly the right spot with their teaching. But the teaching environment also functions as a virtual concert hall and helps to give the young musician the necessary experience of performing.

This mechanism contributes to the success of the famous teachers: their pupils acquire more experience in performing.

In the learning environments of our day, the formerly authoritarian teaching methods have in most cases been replaced by more dialogue-based and individualised teaching. The teacher takes his or her starting point in the student's distinctive character, and the tuition is targeted at the individual.

This is undoubtedly a positive development. The only problem is that dialogue-based teaching does not sufficiently resemble the Concert Hall. Consequently, teaching at the academies should also encompass the conditions that apply at concerts. It is important that the teacher regularly steps back and gives the student the responsibility for his or her own performance by acting as the audience. This does not prevent the teacher providing subsequent dialogue-based guidance and evaluation when the work has been played to the end without interruption.

VIDEO AND AUDIO RECORDINGS

While it has become more difficult for young musicians to gain access to concerts large and small, it has become a great deal easier to create a comprehensive audio or video recording.

Recording yourself is a very effective way of getting a sense of the new reality that arises when we leave the Practice Room and enter the Concert Hall. With audio and video recordings, an effective virtual concert room is created which is characterised by the fact that the musician is now also his or her own audience.

It may seem ridiculous, in a way, that we can build up a concert-like level of psychological excitement just by getting our phone to record what we have been working on; it is hard to see what is at stake, we risk nothing, and we can always just delete the recordings, or not bother watching or listening to them.

The fact that we nonetheless feel exposed – often to the same extent as in a real concert hall – proves in my view my theory that it is not the audience that places us under stress during the concerts, but rather the fact that we cannot simply play the same phrase again if we make an error – we only have one chance. In other words, our state of mind alters radically when we cross the threshold of the Concert Hall.

It is extremely effective to use such a recording to identify elements of imperfections and defects, and then to eliminate them through subsequent targeted practice. But remember that it is lethal for any concert performance if we bring the same type of self-evaluating, critical attitude when performing in the Concert Hall.

In an actual concert, we must shift all our focus away from the precise microscope and centre it on the music and the joy of communicating it.

Making a video can also give us insight into many technical aspects of our musicianship. We might for example discover that a less successful detail may be due to the elbow's positioning, superfluous movements, or an inappropriate posture.

By reviewing a video, we can obtain a more comprehensive picture of how an audience will perceive us: In the video, do I look like a musician that people will want to go out and hear? Do I strike the right balance between extroversion and seriousness? Or are there undesirable details in my demeanour that might distract an audience from my music?

There is the potential for great progress to be made when we make recordings of ourselves, whether we are instrumentalists or singers. Do we make sufficient use of this possibility?

JOINT SESSIONS/THE WORK IN THE CLASSROOM

Joint sessions are a forum in which music students – most often those with the same instrument – gather together and play or sing for each other. Joint sessions should take place with great regularity, and for many music students they are an indispensable part of their academy education.

Joint sessions are also an excellent forum in which to acquire concert training, and they comprise an unusual and stimulating learning environment.

Joint sessions should be held in an informal atmosphere, since the element of competition – when we perform for our fellow students – is highly concrete and can be stressful. Joint sessions are thereby one of the toughest virtual concert halls we have at our disposal.

It is a good idea for everyone in the class, as far as possible, to play at all joint sessions. Not all elements may be equally well-rehearsed but being able to try out even just a part of a studied work is almost as educational as if you have been practising the work for months. The fact that not all of the elements are completely polished also helps to mellow the slightly intense atmosphere that could otherwise arise. You will not be finally judged here on the basis of a less than perfect performance.

Joint sessions have a number of obvious advantages. Because you are playing for your peers – and competitors – a learning space is created here that is at least as intense as at an important concert, audition or examination. The difference is just that here, you share your conditions with all the others, and that you will get another chance in a few weeks' time.

Sometimes the best players in the class do not play as well as they usually do, while the weaker players can have a really good day. A kind of fellowship thus arises which softens up otherwise established hierarchies.

At the joint sessions, everyone gets an opportunity to see how other musicians tackle the tasks. The successful patterns of movement of your fellow students will – consciously or unconsciously – gradually become part of your common musical inheritance. And the often very different versions of the same work will contribute to an understanding of the many alternative possibilities of a given composition.

Joint sessions are also an important place to obtain a good knowledge of the lesser-known repertoire for your instrument. You often acquire better insight into an unknown work at a joint session than if you hear a fully edited recording of it. The performance at a joint session will hardly be as perfect or comprehensive as in a recording, so we are better able to familiarise ourselves with the challenges and assess whether the work lies within our technical capacity, or – quite simply – whether the work appeals to us individually.

It is strongly recommended to make video or audio recordings of the joint sessions. These can also provide an excellent starting point for the next lesson in the principal study. When a student watches his or her own performance on video *together with the teacher*, a unique learning space arises. Perhaps the teacher has for example often pointed out a bad detail in the bowing technique, without the student really managing to correct this – but when the student sees the crooked bowing in a video recording, he or she is motivated in a direct manner to correct it.

A video of the joint session also represents the objectivity that is needed when focus areas are to be prioritised in the teaching. If, for example, stability of tempo is a problem, then *both parties*, by watching the video together, can objectively observe the need for this to be corrected. There may also be issues of intonation, timbre, volume, imagination, fingering or musical charisma.

Joint sessions thus offer their participants useful virtual concert halls. Students who regularly play at joint sessions are undoubtedly better armed against nervousness, better motivated, and better prepared for their concerts, auditions and examinations.

FIND ALTERNATIVE CONCERT FORMS

Playing regularly for other people strengthens every aspect of musicianship. And in passing, we might note that this is really what it's all about. So why not arrange a concert yourself in a café, or a nursing home, a shop, a university aula, a bicycle cellar, a kindergarten, a museum, a park, a metro station or one of the less busy squares in the city?

When classical music is played in unusual places the music reaches new audiences, and this could help to reduce the sense of relative exclusivity and unapproachability that surrounds the classical genre.

A bicycle cellar might for example have fantastic acoustics, and there could be many potentially interested people in the apartment block. But a bicycle cellar has no event manager or budget, so you will have to arrange the concert yourself. It takes daring, time and initiative – but it will usually be worth the trouble and will give you lots of valuable experience.

PROPORTIONS OF THE THREE ROOMS

We know that we need experience in the Concert Hall, but we rarely get all the experience we need. Do we perhaps hesitate too long before entering it?

If this is true, it is due to our reluctance to submit to the "crucial evaluation" that is necessary for a good concert. The Concert Hall is where our own skills and efforts are put to the test, and the assessment of them may be unpleasant, especially if we have not done our best in the Laboratory and the Gym. But when can we say we have done our best?

In the Laboratory, we are free to let ourselves be influenced by all kinds of things, and to change our decisions and perceptions of the music. In the Gym, our freedom is limited to being able to repeat a demanding passage as many times as necessary, until it is securely embedded in our bodies. In both rooms, we are the only ones who judge our work.

In the Concert Hall, however, we are exposed to the evaluation of *both* ourselves and others.

It is my experience, both as a musician and as a teacher, that we spend most of our practice time in the Laboratory, considerably less in the Gym, and least of all in the Concert Hall.

We love the *freedom* of the Laboratory and stay there as long as we can, perhaps for around 70% of our total practice time.

It is more *boring* in the Gym, but since it is here that we have to learn all the things we have decided on, it is my impression that we spend about 20% of our time here.

So, what about the Concert Hall? Here things are really exciting and stimulating, and this is where we can harvest the fruits of our labours with the work in question.

But it is *dangerous* to go in there, because the Concert Hall is the only one of the three rooms in which we risk suffering a defeat. Accordingly, we may only spend around 10% of our time here.

The mental and cognitive benefits of spending time in the Concert Hall are as important and time-consuming as any other exercise. It is simply unwise of us to under-prioritise the vital experience we can gain in the Concert Hall or fail to listen adequately to our own recordings or videos or organise alternative forms of concert.

I believe that the tasks are almost equally great in each of the three rooms, and that if we were to divide our practice time more evenly between the three, i.e. giving around 30% to each, we would be able to significantly strengthen our playing.

WHY DIVIDE UP THE PROCESS SO SHARPLY?

When I have discussed the ideas that underlie *Close the Door Behind You* with students and colleagues I have received a great deal of positive feedback and constructive suggestions, but some people also had some significant reservations.

An often-encountered reservation to this method is that in particular young musicians find it hard to see the point of waiting to sample both the experience and the evaluation of their work until they reach the Concert Hall – after all that laborious and prolonged work in the Laboratory and the Gym.

I can understand that. Why wait to gain the necessary experience with ritualised stages in the practice process, when the world is out there waiting?
In response, I will say two things:

First of all, it is precisely this impatience that is the main reason why we fail to make the necessary decisions about what our own version of the work should be like.

Secondly, we can choose for ourselves how great a portion we will subject to the methodology described. We do not have to go through the entire work or whole movements before we have completed our practice cycle. We are free to select much smaller units – say, half a page or three lines – and apply the methods to these. This requires less patience, but it also poses the risk of the divisions becoming audible and the work losing its homogeneity.

Whether you choose long or short sequences to be the subject of your practising is a matter of individual temperament, but one crucial piece of experience I have gained as a teacher of many years' standing is this: If I ask one of my students to equip their score with detailed, clear and binding directions on technical and musical strategies and decisions, they play better, and their practice goes faster than if they do not decide on these things and note down their decisions.

V. ON REFLECTION

After the concert – whether virtual or real – we will have passed through all three practice rooms. But one important detail is still lacking: evaluation of the overall process.

Even our important concerts are usually only evaluated to a minor extent. A concert being the intense and demanding experience that it is, afterwards we often feel that we would like – at last! – to make a start on a new work. Or just think about something else.

If we do this, however, we miss our very best chance to become better musicians. This is the moment when we have an opportunity to become both wiser and more skilled.

If we take the time to listen to, view or think through the concert, we can gain invaluable insight into both what was successful and what still needs to be improved. The successful parts need to be recognised and expanded in our future work. We often underestimate the importance of noting successful details and wholes. It is misunderstood seriousness on our part to dismiss our positive results as merely basic, banal or obvious. Serious work can just as well consist of expanding successful details as of tackling those that were unsuccessful.

When, after a concert performance, we take the time to evaluate it, there will also be passages that are less successful, if we are honest. Is that why we hesitate to go back and listen to, watch and think through our own concerts? It would be wise for us to note and revise the less successful musical and technical details while they are still fresh in our minds from our work with them in the Laboratory and the Gym.

Another important insight we can gain from listening to our concerts immediately after they have taken place is that passages which in the midst of the concert seemed disastrous might actually be acceptable, while things that felt at the time like minor errors might actually be quite serious. Even highly experienced musicians can often revise their perceptions when they take the time to evaluate their concerts.

The insight that this brings us will provide us with a unique starting point the next time we enter the Laboratory. With the benefit of these new insights and challenges, we can take new decisions in the Laboratory as a basis for renewed practice in the Gym. We will then be ready to play the work again, in some form of Concert Hall.

It will not be a repetition, however, because now we can start our work at a more advanced starting point: a higher level. There will probably be fewer focus points, because all of the successful parts will have been acknowledged and will not need to be revised, and the work will feel easier to play, and to perceive as a conceptual whole. And we can also make use of the new inspiration that we gained in the Concert Hall.

We have moved one level higher up on the spiral staircase of the music. We have completet a positive cyclical proces.

BIBLIOGRAPHY

"Hvorfor er vidensdeling så svært? Om vidensorganisering og læring som kommunikation.", Bang, J.; Heilesen, S. (ed.).

"Mennesket i hjernen, en grundbog i neuropædagogik", Kjeld Fredens, Hans Reitzels forlag, 2012

"Effortless Mastery". Kenny Werner, Alfred Music.

"Einfach Ûben". Gerhardt Mantel, Schott, 2001.

"Does practice make perfect – current theory and research". Harald Jørgensen, Norwegian Academy of Music.

"Musical excellence, strategies and techniques to enhance performance." An anthology compiled by Aaron Williamon, with contributions from, inter alia, Harald Jørgensen, Gary E. McPherson and Emery Schubert.

"Play your Brain", Anette Prehn and Kjeld Fredens, Marshall Cavendish, Business, 2011.

"The Advancing Cellists' Handbook", Benjamin Whitcomb, Authorhouse.

Dr. Noa Kageyama, many articles from the blog "The Bulletproof Musician", e.g. "Why the Progress You Make in the Practice Room Seems to Disappear Overnight".

Tanja Orning· Music as performance – gestures, sound and energy Nov. 2017, in: Journal for Research in Arts and Sports Education

Steen Wackerhausen: "Erfaringsrum, handlingbåren kundskab og refleksion." Refleksion og praksis, Skriftserie nr. 1/2018, Aarhus University

"Tacit and Explicit Knowledge", Harry Collins, University of Chicago Press, Chicago and London, 2010

"Lytning og læsning som kreative processer?", Birgitte Stougaard Pedersen, Peripeti, Tidsskrift for dramaturgiske studier, 2012

"Research and the Self", Morwenna Griffiths, Routledge Companion to Research in the Arts, 2011

Close the Door Behind You
Morten Zeuthen

1st edition · 2019
ISBN: 978-87-87131-08-7

The Royal Danish Academy of Music
Rosenørns Allé 22
1970 Frederiksberg C

Translation: Billy O'Shea
Graphic Design: Kliborg Design
Print: Books on Demand